Published by Pinchback Press
http://www.pinchbackpress.com

"Perfectly Normal" originally appeared in *Perfectly Normal: A Mother's Memoir* by Marcy Sheiner, iUniverse, January 2002.
"Chalk" originally appeared in *Solstice: A Magazine of Diverse Voices*, Fall 2010.
Excerpt from *Some Girls: My Life in a Harem* originally appeared in *Some Girls: My Life in a Harem* by Jillian Lauren, Plume 2010.

Disclaimer and/or Legal Notices: The editors have been told that the stories within this book are true. Names, personal characteristics and traits have been changed to protect the innocent.

Cover and interior illustrations: Linas Garsys
www.linasgarsys.com

Cover and book design: Bonnie Barrett
web.mac.com/stripesandplaid

Editors' Acknowledgements

Thank you to everyone who opens his or her heart on the page. Immense gratitude for my friend/co-editor Cara Bruce, my husband Rich Dolinger, and all who manage to love me in spite of my flaws.

Thanks to Dave Newman for always being there for me and to Shawna Kenney for being a wonderful friend. A special thanks to my family for helping me through my many moments of lost innocence. But, most of all, thanks to everyone who helped us with this book, especially our many talented writers.

Table of Contents

Introduction

What is the age of reason? Not in the sense of an era, but in a person's life? We learn from watching those around us, doing as we're told, seeing the world through the lens of our parents. But that lens must always crack. Some pebble of truth penetrates the shield of reality our family has so carefully built around us. Then the lens shatters and we see things anew, through our own eyes. Moment by moment, event by event, we become our own beings with our own truths. For some, loss of innocence comes with learning how to lie. Others may discover religion, love, success, sex or honesty come with a price.

My own naiveté has been challenged in a series of moments. As a child, when I witnessed a teacher being unusually cruel or a relative making a racist joke or some other adult making an unjust decision, I realized something important: adults could be wrong. These authority figures that seemed to know so much sometimes really knew nothing; the rules I had been so dutifully memorizing were sometimes being made up as we went along. The rules were arbitrary and fake. The rules did not always apply.

I rebelled. Often the ones I pushed hardest against were those I loved the most, the ones I had expected so much more from. My father was a harsh disciplinarian, an opinionated man, judgmental of the changing world around him. In his death, I suddenly understood frailty. He, too, had been hurt and disappointed. And despite his faults, he had also been brave, loving and kind. Why did it take his exit from this world for me to learn forgiveness? None of us can always play hero or villain. The world is not black and white. We live in shades of grey.

The human heart breaks but heals again and again. This fact inspires me. I'd like to think my innocence is never lost. The world is full of wonder. I am wiser, but still enamored.

Shawna Kenney, 2011

Most of us recognize the moments when our lives changed direction. We are not always aware of these moments while they are occurring, often it isn't until months or even years later when we trace our current situation back and realize *that* was when things changed. If we had made a different choice, chosen a different path, we might now be in a different place. However some moments are too clear—these often-called epiphanies or awakenings.

I don't believe that innocence can be lost from merely watching; instead, the loss must come from experience, from living through one of these life changing moments, no matter how big or how small, and coming out, more or less intact, on the other side. We make a choice and we survive, forever different and forever changed.

I do believe that loss of innocence doesn't happen all at once. Our pleasant world view isn't shattered by one moment. It takes many as our innocence chips away slowly. When I think about my own loss of innocence there are so many of these times. In my life I've experienced death, sex, war, poverty, violence, disease and too much regret to even keep track of. Not all of these were done *to* me; I have made many bad choices and suffered the consequences. And each of these events has shaped me, molded me, and caressed me, eroding my innocence like a stone in a river. Yet, I still believe that I have some innocence left. I like to believe that we all do. That these events don't stain us completely; we might be a little dirty, but we can still clean up okay.

These stories are about such moments. Events that occurred at all ages: loss of a sibling, arrest of a father, sex or lack of it, attentions from an older man, finding out a hard truth, learning a painful lesson. These stories may not be what you expect. They aren't all tragedies, in fact, some are quite funny. These are the true stories of experience, of those moments we will never forget.

Cara Bruce, 2011

Invoice for My Virginity

By Amanda Kingsbury

Dear Shawn:

Thank you for your business as of August 1988. I would gladly extend the courtesy of saying the pleasure was all mine, but that wouldn't be entirely accurate, as this correspondence will further make clear. Nor do I believe that expressing such false gratitude will lessen the shock of this invoice—particularly if your wife is the one who pays the bills. In any event, let me reassure you that I am not initiating a lawsuit, so there is no need for anyone to contact the family attorney.

Should a legal dispute arise, however, I have taken great care to itemize. How I arrived at the sum of $17,675 for my virginity is more exacting than it seems. For instance, there was a $200 charge for the ridiculous blond mustache you grew—the one that made you look like a rural Wisconsin patrol officer—after I expressly told you that I hated facial hair. And another $150 for announcing that you were "upstairs, pinching a loaf" when I arrived at your apartment the next afternoon and called out,

"Shawn, where are you?" I might have only charged $100, but you said it in that creepy cartoon voice of Peter Lorre.

Yes, the base fee of $10,000 is somewhat arbitrary. But it's the extras—isn't it always?—that drive up the cost. And I extended considerable savings by not charging interest, which would have been compounded over 19 years.

So, then, to continue breaking it down in no particular order: I assessed a $1,000 fee for your post-coital theatrics: dismounting with exaggerated athletic flair after we completed the inaugural act, flexing your biceps and boasting, "I am the Hy-Men-A-Tor." At least you made a good-faith effort at foreplay, though your clumsy insert ($350) did make me wince considerably. I'm not sure how or why you later persuaded me to be on top; it seems rather adventurous and potentially injurious for a first timer. But then again, those two strawberry wine coolers you brought over did go a long way toward dissolving my inhibitions.

Of course, a certain amount of incredulity is to be expected. I was a 17-year-old virgin eager to have sex, and what strapping 21-year-old Midwestern boy turns that down on principle? And yes, you could argue that it was premeditated on my part. I did kick my friends out of my parents' house that night. But you, too, anticipated that it was finally going to happen, despite your best efforts to present an illusion of spontaneity. You showered in Drakkar ($50), put on a nice T-shirt and arrived with your signature romantic mix tape. Apparently it never occurred to you that despite my willingness, the timing may have been unseemly, as my father was in the hospital, recovering from a serious heart attack. (He's fine now.)

And though the specific experience itself was satisfying in a frozen pizza kind of way, and I made the requisite primal moans, you still had the audacity to ask, "Did you cum?" ($400). You know I despise that word.

You see, it simply occurred to me one day about a year ago—while sitting in the Starbucks drive-thru with a red wine headache—that I did not have to give my virginity away for free when there are young women auctioning off their maidenheads to the highest bidder. (Not to mention, terrorists executing suicide missions in hopes of procuring 72 virgins, or white raisins, depending on whose scholarly interpretation you consult.) The last time I checked, that graduate student from San Diego had a going rate of $3.8 million, all for the honor of piercing a negligible set of soft tissues whose anatomical function is, at best, questionable. And then there was that Bristol University student who put her virtue on eBay a few years ago and said she'd rather sleep with a stranger once than spend years paying off her student loans. Perhaps if I had submitted this invoice in a more timely fashion—the summer I left for college—I could have avoided 10 years of monthly payments to Sallie Mae, or upgraded from a middling university to private liberal arts college. But I digress; this is not a bid for salary recompense.

Admittedly, we did have fun that summer. You could actually be a gentleman, like the night we dry-humped in the backseat of your car behind that cabinetry warehouse. You started to unzip your jeans when I stopped you and said, "Shawn, I'm a virgin."

"Really?" you asked, and started to re-do your pants.

Then you paused, as if unconvinced. "Really?" ($225). You reassured me, though, that we didn't have to do anything, and we continued steaming up the windows of your Honda. And then you lamented that you hadn't seen an intact vagina in five years, and would I at least oblige you with a close-up view, and that led to my first nether-region contact with a beer-chilled tongue. It was a somewhat prosaic experience, as I recall, and it caused me to wonder if I had a defective clitoris ($300). That was before I realized that you were simply the first in a long line of men who would fail to rock my world.

But after that night, I didn't hear from you for another week. When I ran into you at Seeberger's party, talking to that tall blond, you tried to convince me that you'd been busy with work ($425 + $75 because you clearly knew of my insecurity surrounding willowy blonds with Nordic noses). It was at that point I realized our relationship would require the bond of sex if it were to continue through the summer. More than that, I was tired of being the only virgin in my circle of friends, and I wanted to relieve myself of the burden of holding out for "the right guy."

And so, given the sluggish emotional indifference on both of our parts, I did not expect tenderness. Yet you had to ruin it by whispering, "I love you," upon (your) climax. Please. You were still thinking about Pam. Because afterward you said to me, "You didn't bleed. Pam bled a lot." ($1,500) I apologize if you had plans of parading our soiled sheets down the street. Besides, I technically ruptured myself at age 14, when I fell off my bike in front of Dairy Queen. It was excruciating, even more so because I had a sizeable audience.

But the baffling behavior that secured the highest fee is the fact that you seemed to assume that because you were "my first," you earned unquestioning lifetime access ($3,000). That night at Indiana University, when I ran into you at that party, I had to lock myself in Molly's car and burrow into the backseat to escape your obsessive advances. I lay there for some 40 minutes, nearly suffocating in the heat, while you banged on the window, until you finally slumped against the rear driver's seat door and passed out.

After I graduated, you looked me up at my first job, and when I reluctantly met you for a drink, you would not relent—despite the fact that I told you I had a semi-serious boyfriend. And Gina tells me you were back home a few months ago, drunkenly confessing, "I should have never let that one go."

I appreciate any concern you may have for my financial well-being, but I assure you, this is not a plea for a loan. Unlike many of my later friends, I never felt the need to reclaim my "second virginity," to erase the guilt of bad judgment or take control of my virtue. It's just that over the years, I have realized that purity, indeed, has its price. In some countries, it's murder. In Deuteronomy, it is 50 silver shekels, paid to the unbetrothed woman's father. On Gigimo, the Chinese sex-toy Web site, it's $29.50. At least that's how much it costs to obtain the "artificial virginity hymen," a plastic baggie filled with mysterious red goop meant to resemble the chaste secretions of a newly deflowered virgin. (You can even pick up "liquid virgin," applied 15 minutes before sex, to facilitate the "pucker.")

Again, I thank you for your business. Perhaps I will

establish an agency called Cherry Chasers, to collect payment on behalf of other women like me, who simply did not realize the financial power that intact virtue could bring. As such, I would appreciate prompt, in-full payment. Otherwise, I might have to sic my "Poon Goons" on you—ha ha.

Seriously, please remit now.

Regards,

Amanda

Breaking My Silence (Among Other Things)

By Jennifer D. Munro

I wanted to hop in the sack, but I got the sack instead. Dark and lusty romance novel heroes go to great lengths to corrupt innocent heroines, but my boyfriends all split as soon as they heard that they would be my "first." I had passed the legal age limit for drinking and voting, so my dates didn't think they had an intact hymen to contend with. I think my potty mouth fooled them; how could a girl who talked a foul blue streak *not* have rolled in the gutter? I was anxious to discard the nun's habit of chastity, but my beaux high-tailed it as soon as they learned that sex with me would have actual significance. They thought they heard the knell of wedding chimes, but I just wanted them to ring my bell. How hard could it be (very, I hoped)? I wasn't asking for an orgasm, even: just a handy tool to knock down my last barricade to adult wisdom.

No moral code kept me unsullied all those years. I subscribed to no religion. What can I say? I got my nose stuck in a book and adolescence passed me by. I'd tarnish my virtue later. Just let me finish this chapter first. But like any Jane Austen heroine, I sensed time ticking—time to retire the library card and check out real life experience before I became the bitter, sex-deprived witch of fairy tales. As I began my senior year of college, I decided that I would lower my drawbridge for the first decent Lancelot who knocked with raised spear. I couldn't possibly be saddled with my maidenhead when I was handed my bachelor's degree. Even my mother in the fifties had gotten the dirty deed over with before starting college (my brother being one result).

I had no trouble finding prospective candidates. A parade of knights had been there all along while I'd been dog-earing pages instead of howling at the moon. Sure, I could have had a one-night stand with a stranger. But I was enough of a romantic that I wanted my first lover to remember my name in the morning. I wanted us to feel each other out before he felt me up. Like getting lost in the world of a good book, hooked from page one to *denouement*, I fell in love with each of these boys as we dated and danced our way towards the dirty deed. But while books involved a climax, my love life didn't. I had the urge to merge, but my boyfriends kept taking the off ramp.

Stud chose me as his bad girl on the side. A born-again Christian, Stud wrestled with memories of pre-conversion pleasures. Officially he dated Prim, a proper woman of faith. For me, Stud revealed his dark side, teaching me fancy Top Ramen recipes, advising me to eat the core along with the apple, and discussing U2 music as if it was Leviticus. Stud and I skipped rapidly down the path toward fornication, until he leaned over at a party and snorted white stuff up his nostrils. He'd thought I'd been around the block a few times and would join him for a few lines before we rolled in the hay. When it turned out that I was as pure as the snow up his nose, he took off. If he was going to have to be delicate with a virgin, it would at least be one who earned him some celestial points, not another black mark against his afterlife. He went back to Prim, praying I wouldn't tell her that he got lit on more than altar candles. Poor Stud got it all backwards. Prim had lost hers a long time ago on more than tampons and horseback riding. Like many a fictional heroine, I was completely misunderstood, and the bad prince trotted off with the wrong wench.

Alas, my unoccupied apartment still needed a tenant. But after years of vacancy, folks suspected there must be something wrong with the premises—hauntings, vermin, old carpeting. But I put out a new sign and accepted the next applicant.

I loved words, so Mustache was a good bet for my second try since he read me Emily Dickinson poetry late into the night. With his obsession for maid-to-the-grave (or was she?) Emily, his potential kink for virgins was made to order. Stud was a real looker (although I'm gleeful to note that premature balding had already begun to rear its ugly head), but maybe I'd have better luck with the more average looking Mustache. Intending to become a sports medicine doctor, he was passionate about the creak in my knees, and we groped our way towards eventual copulation. Mustache had also accepted Jesus after experimenting with most forms of deviancy during a stint in the armed forces. You'd think my treasure would be easier to find than God, but the man upstairs worked in mysterious ways. I was obviously attracted to the conflicted misery of these soul-searching boys, tormented by wavering faith and bad eighties hair, but I'd waited too long. My potential paramours had already tried everything (except me), and were ready to cool off while my teakettle had just started to whistle. One night Mustache learned that he'd flunked his pre-med exam. He guzzled a bottle of expensive Russian vodka that he'd been saving—for what, I'm not sure, but failure obviously qualified. Then he unceremoniously maneuvered into blow job position. I said that's not where I wanted it, because I had this other nagging thing I needed to get rid of. Mustache ricocheted off of me and hit the wall on the other side of the room like I'd said I had V.D., not Virginity. At that point, Mustache confessed that he had a wife. I was another cross that he could not bear. God had set me in his path to keep him from crossing back to the dark side, and I should get me back to the nunnery.

Any human resources expert will tell you that the long-unemployed person has a harder time finding a job than the applicant who is still working: résumés with long gaps in employment history cause suspicion. The firm speculates on the candidate's flaws rather than concentrating on her strengths. But I hit the pavement again, seeking gainful fulfillment.

Near as I can figure it, the problem with Pasty was that he was still a virgin, too. Nice guy. We hung out for awhile, scuffing our toes in the dirt of first base, each waiting for the other one to steal second. Neither one of us made a move. Around the seventh inning stretch, we shook hands like good sports and left the field. We'd both try to hit a home run with someone else.

The longer you keep something, the harder it is to get rid of it. Take that horrific tchotchke from Aunt Alice that you can't quite put in the Goodwill bag. Yet everyone around me was giving away their virtue without qualm. My gay guy friend slept with my straight girlfriend, just to get it out of the way. Same with my lesbian friend sleeping with my straight (or was he?) guy friend, although, between you and me, he seemed a little big for the job. But while cherries were popping wildly around me in the heat of carefree passion, my oven never got past preheat.

Hairy was at least honest. He said he simply didn't want the baggage of being my first. His first time had been a disaster, and he didn't want that potential weight hanging around his karma. He said I should go have bad sex with somebody else. He at least gave me an orgasm for the road. "Put it in the bank," he said. "You'll need it." Hairy refused to hold my hand in public. He said he was uncomfortable with public displays of affection, but it turned out that he feared the other three girls he was screwing would catch him with me. So much for honesty.

Eve sure had it easy. Temptation was nowhere in sight, until I met a man with a real live snake. I chose a scientist, figuring God wouldn't be nipping at his heels. Geek adored his cold-blooded pet. But after I watched a live mouse go down the reptile's gullet, right next to the bed, I reevaluated my immediate need for a serpent in my life and sssaid sssayonara.

So I graduated with a near perfect GPA and an illiterate G-spot. I entered the job market *cum laude* with a lonely yoni.

The irony of it all is that when, a year later, I finally slept with the man who would become my husband, I was forced to lie: I told him that I was still a virgin, which I no longer was. Let's call it Extenuating Circumstances. We dated for a couple of months, but he lived in the submariners' barracks, and I had moved back in with my folks after graduation. Twin bed, horse stickers on the headstand, parents snoring in the next room. Future Husband and I fumbled our way toward the whole nine yards, but with public beaches as our only trysting fields, the only thing that made a touchdown was sand (which proved harder to get rid of than my virginity). Future Husband knew he'd be my first, if we could figure out where to do it, but he was unfazed not only by the unruptured state of my previous affairs but by having to wait as we dealt with logistics. Finally, a man not intimidated by my accidental celibacy. Definitely the kick in the pants I needed to get my own apartment, where we could consummate our "why not?" level of mutual affection; this was about the birds and the bees, not love and rockets. But a week before I moved in to a hovel with yellow-paisley furniture (it had a queen-sized bed, and nothing else mattered), Future Husband went home on leave and got in an accident on the other side of the country. The emergency room doctor proclaimed that he would be a vegetable for the rest of his life. Now I'd call this going to great lengths to avoid besmirching my vestal robe. The chastity belt tightened with another approaching birthday, yet I had already lost my innocence with the unexpected phone call announcing his awful and unexpected fate. For as long as I'd retained my hymen, I'd also maintained my idealistic and simplistic notion of the world and its fairness. Other than distant events like the explosion of the Space Shuttle Challenger, I had been as untouched by tragedy as by boys. While he was not the man of my dreams and we were not in love, Future Husband had been decent and kind about a millstone that crushed my prurient plans with the young men who came before him. He was young, his life full of possibility as he drove his VW Bug with the top down, yearning to be a high school art teacher when he got out of the military. Now he would never drive or draw again, senselessly because he was in the wrong place at the wrong time, and I would never see him again. My notion of the world was tainted although my virtue wasn't.

My girlfriend and I took a long-planned vacation to a U.S. Naval base in Japan, where her father was stationed. I thought I would be rubbing Buddhas, traipsing around temples with my friend's mother, but I ended up rubbing shoulders with hundreds of scared and lonely sailors—many not long out of high school—about to set sail for the Persian Gulf. We were the only white, civilian women for barb-wired miles. The proper local women wouldn't give the sailors the time of day. Who was I to withhold consolation? We flicked our Bics and sang to Bon Jovi at the enlisted man's club, where six pink *frou frou* drinks arrived in front of me before I even finished my first. I wore a white Laura Ashley dress. I was treated like a Lady, and my garden needed tending. Desperation on all sides crept beneath the alcoholic hilarity, but the fact remained that I had my pick of boys who were ready, willing, and able to deflower me. There was something fitting to the pall cast over this momentous moment by the specter of war, loneliness, tragedy, and young lives squandered, both here and back home.

I chose a lovely, kind boy who pawned his watch in exchange for a guitar so he could serenade me on the streets of Yokusuka. On a romantic date, he slew my dragons of doubt and disloyalty to Future Husband by facing down a meal of raw fish to impress me. We scraped and borrowed money to rent a by-the-hour room for the night in the Love Motel with a miniature Statue of Liberty on the roof. The coincidental metaphor didn't escape me. When it was over, Lovely Boy asked me how I felt. "Relieved," I answered. He was hoping for something more profound, but for me, the moment couldn't have been deeper. More than a fleeting rite of passage that had never much interested me, it satisfied a yearning to live life fully, to connect, before chance and ill luck severed possibility. He gave me his dog tag, souvenir of the night he barked up my tree.

After I returned home, Lovely Boy and I exchanged passionate letters. He planned to visit me during his upcoming leave. Since the ice between us had already been broken (among other things), we weren't shy in our correspondence about what we planned to do together. The deposit on my new apartment would not turn out to be a waste.

Then, unexpectedly, a shuffling and slurring Future Husband returned. He looked like he'd just woken up from a coma, which is exactly what he'd done. How could I have the heart to confess to him about Lovely Boy? "Darling, while you were hooked up to tubes I let the first sniffing biped who came along take a dip in my honey pot. Sorry, but I thought your future involved diapers, not condoms." It would have been indecent to break up with a man who couldn't remember that he was a vegetarian (to his Midwestern mother's delight), how to knot his necktie, or common words such as "car" (which he coined "people mover") or "potato chip" ("crunchy flats"). Lovely Boy's visit loomed closer. Florence Nightingale wouldn't abandon Dopey for Prince Charming, so I told Lovely Boy to cancel his trip. I had been honest with him about Future Husband's presence in the background all along, and Lovely Boy respected my decision, which was not an easy one. While one lover was traveling to what was quickly becoming a war zone, the other suffered a war with his own injured body. I could not simply dump him because an able understudy had stepped in to take his role. *This* was virtue, not what was or wasn't intact between my legs, and this virtue I planned to keep.

Lovely Boy and I agreed to be friends, but I never heard from him again. According to the wilting grapevine, he was dishonorably discharged from the Navy some time later after attempting, in a drunken stupor, to break into the house where I'd been staying, calling out for me to make him breakfast— so I'd made a narrow escape from life with Fred Flintstone. Unfortunately, I let his sleeping dog tag lie and it came back to bite me in the butt. Only one other thing from the fairy tale evening with Lovely Boy remains: the bladder infection I got after that night has lasted about twenty years.

Future Husband and I slept together soon after, a

complicated coupling owing to his dizzy spells. We did it on the itchy, mustard-yellow carpet so we wouldn't fall off the vinyl couch if he swooned. I couldn't bring myself to admit to him that someone else's family jewels had sparkled in my vault while his had been rusting away. He was gentle with me (not surprisingly, since his waking state at that point was half asleep), but I didn't have to fake the virgin stuff, because, frankly, it still hurt. Not long after, he discovered Lovely Boy's letters and dog tag, and he worried the truth out of me. Feeling betrayed, he broke up with me. That took the cake. All those guys cutting loose from my virginal mother lode, and now Future Husband was ditching me because I'd gone and lost it with someone else. Desperation had led to drastic measures while he'd been on life support, and I persuaded Future Husband (not difficult in his head-injured state) that the night with Lovely Boy was a technicality that didn't count. I still believe this is true, having experienced the difference between *making love* and *having sex*. I also told Future Husband that he was better and bigger; that smoothed things over, and he moved in with me (that he had nowhere else to go tipped the odds in my favor).

Dopey eventually recovered most of his brain synapses and blossomed into a passable Prince Charming. I never set out to lose my virginity with my soul mate, but after two decades with my Past, Present, and Future Husband, I guess I did. I tried for years without success to *get lucky*, but once he snapped out of it and started using words like "paradigm" and "pedagogy" on me, I assure you that he counted it as *his* lucky night.

Now in my forties, I find the tardy loss of my virginity to be my dirtiest secret. Amongst intimate and casual friends alike who divulge sordid details of affairs, abortions, same-sex experiments, shoplifting, cross-dressing, sleeping with their therapists, putting recyclables in with the trash, and forgetting the boss's time-sensitive FedEx package in the restroom, I find my long-intact hymen and lifelong monogamy impossible to confess. I feel actual shame in my lack of sexual congress until I nearly hit the quarter century mark. It's like I wet the bed, not that I kept my virginity until I had almost surpassed the lifespan of linoleum. Like Stud and his misconception of my track record, I've come full circle; my current friends and acquaintances are deluded about my past experience. I've earned a reputation by proxy, as an erotica writer, gutter talker, motorcycle mama, and hip-flask bearer. Even my mother thinks I lost it long before I did, back with Hairy. I have no excuse. Long after the Age of Aquarius set us free, I was still treading water. I came of age in the wild and carefree eighties, when the eye-shadowed boys of Duran Duran hung off the side of a speeding yacht without life preservers. Sexual barriers had all been broken. Boys wore makeup and girls were athletes. We had The Pill, and AIDS was just a rumor. And there I was, playing the French Horn and reading *The Iliad*.

I was not a God-fearing woman, living a church-prescribed choice of virginity until marriage. Sex was simply irrelevant to who I was as a person. The hymen, after all, is just a mucous membrane. Perhaps I intuited that a cultural mythology involving mucous was not worth getting uptight about and was also about as arousing as the Michael Jackson-Lisa Marie Presley kiss. Or perhaps I intuited that my technical virginity was the least of what I had to lose. With sexual knowledge came firsthand experience of a complicated world that I would have preferred to keep as fiction between the pages of a book—a novel that I could close when the plot got too intense. As Lovely Boy passed dull and fearful hours in the Persian Gulf and Future Husband learned to walk and write (and fornicate) again, Honest Hairy surprised me with a late night phone call. He had tracked me down to make sure he could prepare me before I heard the news: his friend Pasty, the sweet boy who couldn't screw up the courage to put the moves on me, had hanged himself. I choose to believe that he hanged himself on purpose in a moment of overwhelming depression rather than Hairy's understanding that Pasty died by accident during erotic asphyxiation. While neither scenario is cheerful, I can't square the desperation of such lonely sexual deviancy with the skittish virgin boy that I knew.

Instead of remembering him in a humiliating state of *dishabille* swinging from the rafters of his garage, I choose to remember him as he was on our carefree drive to the coast in his convertible Karmann Ghia, top down, his badly-cut mop of brown hair flying straight up in the wind, the pair of us innocent virgins, happy, with everything in the world left to lose.

Candy Arm

By Jennifer Rhodes

She has the best rack I've ever seen.

As I sit ogling it, I ponder whether they are real. If they are, I am jealous and curse God for giving her the kind of chest that makes even girls stare and giving me nothing more than two overgrown mosquito bites.

If they are not real, I contemplate asking her if I could feel them.

I'm dying to know what implants feel like. What *her* implants feel like. Are they like water balloons gently sloshing beneath the skin? Do they harden like rocks or warp like an unfinished wood floor, contorting, rippling?

I'm sitting next to her in class, supposed to be listening, but I can't. I cannot take my eyes off of her. I study her. I analyze her.

When I walked into the room I noticed she was there, almost immediately. My heart stopped.

"Is anyone sitting here?" I asked.

"You are," she said, moving her bag.

The cocoon in my stomach tore open; the butterflies violently flapped their wings.

I get to sit next to her, I thought. And the longer I sat, the more I thought. *This will make me important by association. Everyone knows her, admires her. The other students in the room will see me sitting next to her, assume we are friends and hold me in the same esteem.* The awe and admiration I will attract for being perceived of as her friend, for being perceived as being like her will make me content.

Will make me enough.

Will make it okay to be me.

I've watched her from afar for awhile now. Her long hair swishes when she walks, flowing gently down her back like a terracotta waterfall. She has these translucent blue eyes and when she looks at you she sees you—she really *sees* you—making you feel like you are the only other person in the room. When she is not concentrating on school she is smiling, talking, everyone seems to know her. Everything about her is authentic—her leather motorcycle jacket is not a fashion statement; she really rides a bike. She does not teach pole dancing classes because it's the newest fad; she actually is a dancer. She walks confidently, gallantly, balancing strength with beauty; a level head with a free spirit.

The professor lectures, but my focus remains unchanged. She is oblivious to me, engaged in the lecture, her fingers clicking away at the keys of her laptop as she takes notes. I strain to read them, to get into her head and see how she thinks. Does she write down what the professor says verbatim or does she paraphrase? I can't really see.

I look around the classroom to see if anyone notices who I'm sitting next to.

If anyone is trying to read *my* notes.

If anyone is transfixed on me, fascinated, silently thinking *I wonder if she had a breast reduction, and if so, I'd like to feel them.*

No one is looking.

I look at her again, studying her features, taking in her unconventional perfection.

I want to be like that.

I want to be her.

I see her chest rise and fall as she breathes and wish that when she exhales her confidence would waft out so I could inhale it. Then, I think, I'd know what it feels like to be happy. Then, I think, I could be more like her.

If I were more like her it would be okay to be me.

She can feel the weight of my stare and turns toward me. I smile, embarrassed.

I am such a fuck up, I think to myself. *Who does that? Who stares at people with crazy, mad intensity like that? What are you doing? That's what psychos do! Psychos and stalkers and pedophiles!*

I go back to scanning the room.

Still, no one is looking at me.

I look out the window, just over her shoulder, wishing to be sucked up into the ominous clouds that loom overhead.

***

We've only really ever spoken twice. The first time was

last June during a lecture at school. She caught me staring at her and I explained, red faced, that I was just studying her tattoos, the two full sleeves that decorate her toned arms. She smiled and nodded as if this had happened many times before. One arm, she explained, was her "candy arm". Upon closer inspection I saw that it was whimsically covered, shoulder to wrist, with pastel-colored candies reminiscent of childhood. A Peep chick, Starlight mints, a scattering of Candy Corn, a spoonful of sugar. She smiled, a kind, genuine smile, and went back to her work. I racked my brain to think of something to say, some way of extending the conversation, but the moment had passed.

I would refer to this conversation repeatedly over the next six months. Every time I talked to someone with a tattoo, I felt compelled to bring her up. *I go to school with a girl and she has a candy arm,* I'd say.

Once when my husband and I were out to dinner our server had a large tattoo draping across her cleavage. I remember her chest was definitely real, the kind of breasts that probably hit the floor when she takes off her bra. I would not touch them with a ten-foot pole. I don't remember what her tattoo said.

"I like your tattoo," I told her.

This was not true.

My husband had heard this many times over the past few months. He rolled his eyes. He knew what was coming next.

"She knows someone who has a candy arm," he said dryly. "A sleeve with candy on it." He said this as if he was no longer amused, or maybe was never amused by it in the first place.

The server smiled, a phony waitress-smiling-for-tips smile,

pretending to be interested.

The second time we spoke was six months later. A classmate formally introduced us because of our shared passion for pole dancing.

"Look! I have both your pole dancing pictures on my computer!" The classmate opened her laptop, excitedly pointing and clicking to retrieve the saved images.

"No. Really. Don't pull those up…" I stammered. I didn't want her to see me. See what a loser I am, see us contrasted like that.

On one side of the screen: a professional, pinup-esque shot of her on the pole; her penetrating gaze staring out of the photo, a coy smirk crossing her sultry red lips. Her deep red hair set in curls cascading elegantly over her shoulder.

On the other side: me in my run-down apartment's living room the day my pole arrived. I am grinning like an overzealous five-year-old on Christmas morning as I dangle like an amateur from the newly set up pole, playing up to the camera in ratty gym shorts and a tank top.

"That's very good." She nodded at me in approval.

I couldn't understand how she could be so genuinely nice about a picture that was so genuinely awful. While her picture was reminiscent of Bettie Page, mine looked like the white-trash stripper they stick in the corner at the local dive, the scrawny, ugly one who has to resort to blow jobs to earn her rent because she's got no tits. The one who attracts comments like "Is them there titties all ya got? Take this here twenty and go getcha some fake ones. When ya getcha some titties you can come dance for me 'cuz I'd sure like ta feel 'em"

***

My whole life I played by the rules.

I did my homework in high school and got into a good university, where I joined a sorority, as expected. I wore my hair the way everyone else did. I wore the clothes that *Glamour* said I should. I gave head the way *Cosmo* said I was supposed to. I was careful not to raise any eyebrows or take any risks. There were chances I wanted to take, lives I wanted to try out, but I squelched the thoughts as soon as they entered my head. Because nice Jewish girls do not get tattoos. Nice Jewish girls do not become strippers. Nice Jewish girls do not go down on other girls. Nice Jewish girls do not sleep with black football players. Nice Jewish girls do not learn to play the drums and join rock bands.

In college I learned my place and played it well; nice Jewish girls snort lines of coke up their cosmetically altered noses. They forcibly throw up after eating and have one night stands with frat boys. Then they get married and refrain from attracting attention. So I honed my edges, grinding them down, smoothing the corners, trying to be that puzzle piece that fits perfectly into the center of the picture.

But, at 29, playing by the rules has gotten me nowhere.

I do not have a career—I barely even have a job. I do not own a house. I do not own my car. My bank accounts are empty. I sit home on Friday nights because I have no friends. My voicemail never registers that I have a message. My only emails are from Amazon.com reminding me that my books are on the way. I ground myself down to the point where I am not sharp enough to fit into my fantasy world, yet no matter how hard I try to jam myself into the real world I do not fit into that puzzle either. I don't fit in anywhere.

And for everything I am, she is the opposite. She dared to take the risks I did not and lived the life I wanted to live. The desires I pushed out of my mind, she embraced. The chances I was too afraid to take, she grabbed. The experiences I will never have are tucked safely away in her memory. She refused to compromise her many angles and complexities, but seamlessly fits in anywhere. She got the tattoos. Became the exotic dancer. She rubs elbows with rock stars and artists and iconoclastic writers. She wears her hair the way she wants to, wears the clothes she likes, gives head to whomever she wants, without a magazine dictating which way her tongue should move. She didn't play by the rules but shattered them into a million tiny pieces.

A million tiny pieces. Like my dreams. Like the life I wanted. Like the life I could have had.

The life she's lived is recorded on her arm: whimsical, colorful, sweet.

My arm is ashen. Pasty. Dull.

***

I see her in the hallway of school just before I leave to fly back to Ohio.

"I'm writing a story about you." I blurt this out before I even realize what I'm doing. Immediately I wish I'd said nothing. I want to disappear. I look down at the floor, willing it to open up and swallow me. It doesn't.

She smiles graciously and tells me she is flattered.

"I'll let you see it as soon as it's finished," I say. Then I sheepishly hurry out the double doors into the courtyard.

And I wonder what happens next.

I wonder if she will know that she matters to me, that she inspires me. I wonder if someone with such ample confidence and abundant beauty could ever notice someone as flat and empty as me.

And I wonder if I will ever have my own candy arm; a candy arm as stunning and brilliant as hers.

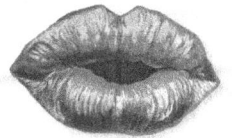

Perfectly Normal

By Marcy Sheiner

August 3, 1965. I awoke to find myself in a room with a woman sitting up in the bed next to mine, pulling metal rollers out of her long brown hair.

"Hi," she said cheerily. "My name's Jackie. God, am I glad for some company. Now that I'm leaving tomorrow they finally bring someone in here. Isn't it always the way?"

I smiled uncertainly through a sodium pentathol induced haze.

"I had a boy too," Jackie continued. "They'll be coming around for feeding soon. You'd better let the nurse know you're up if you want to see yours."

I rang for the nurse.

"Oh, so you're up, Mama. Have you urinated or had a BM yet?"

I shook my head, remembering my sister Linda's vivid descriptions of the excretion ceremonies on the maternity ward; I knew if I didn't urinate they'd catherize me, an altogether unpleasant affair, and that I wouldn't be allowed to leave the hospital until I'd emptied my bowels.

I strained on the bedpan, examining my body. My belly was loose and flabby, still patterned by purple stretch marks: so, I was stuck with them for life. My vagina was a pathetic mess, having been not only assaulted by a razor, but cut and stitched as well, episiotomies being as much a routine of childbirth as cutting the umbilical cord.

"Have you done it yet?" called the nurse.

"Not yet."

"Well, dear, I'm going to have to catherize you."

Threatened with invasion, my bladder immediately released a healthy stream of urine. When the nurse returned with her equipment, she actually seemed disappointed.

"And now are you mommies ready for your babies?" she asked. Jackie and I nodded eagerly.

My newborn son slept in a tiny glass box perched atop four wheeled legs. At first sight he resembled my grandfather, or any old man, his red face scrunched up in denial of his new surroundings. The nurse gave him to me with a bottle of water. He took a few weak sucks, then fell back asleep. Jackie's baby sucked avidly.

"Don't worry," she assured me. "Mine didn't drink the first day either."

Holding Daryl, I felt far older than my 19 years. For the first time I questioned my decision not to breast-feed—I had thought it old-fashioned, an activity suitable only for cows, an attitude that was enthusiastically endorsed by my family, friends, and doctor. Well, it was too late now—I'd been given pills to dry up my milk.

Surreptitiously I unfolded the blanket and took a quick inventory: ten toes, ten fingers, all in the right places. One tiny limp penis. Relieved, I closed my eyes and leaned against the pillow.

Jackie's voice startled me. "Aren't you glad he's all right? I was terrified something would be wrong with my baby. But thank God, he's perfectly normal."

"Yes." I breathed, recalling the nightmares: attacks on my swollen stomach, hideous creatures clinging to my vaginal walls.

In the evening, visitors filled our room. Jackie's husband and mother stood quietly by her bed, while my mother, father, husband and sister filled up the rest of the space. My family tends to make a scene wherever they go, and this was no exception. Jackie's visitors gaped openly as my mother held forth, loudly commenting on everything from the hospital decor to the staff.

Bob had brought a bouquet of roses, and Linda ran off in search of a vase. When she returned she made a great fuss with them, searching for a knife to cut the stems, filling the vase, arranging them just so. This domesticity was totally out of character; I kept wanting my older sister to sit down and commiserate with me about the maternity ward, but she seemed to be avoiding any intimacy.

Bob's face was covered with thick stubble, rendering his dark skin even darker. He slouched in the corner chair next to my bed, inexplicably subdued.

My father grinned from ear to ear, and my mother sported her usual stiff smile, worn through thick and thin—but I had the uneasy sense that they were disappointed in me. Maybe it was because I'd had a boy—in my family we coveted female babies as dolls to dress up and show off.

Everything was discordant. Feeling acutely uncomfortable, I suddenly had to go to the bathroom—a tedious event that included pouring a pitcher of water over my stitched bottom in lieu of toilet paper, a procedure which everyone in the room could not avoid hearing. I should have been embarrassed, but I wasn't; the bathroom afforded me an escape from a claustrophobic atmosphere that I couldn't identify.

The next morning my obstetrician, a young crew-cutted fellow with an upturned nose and pasty skin came in to check on me. As he poked at my breasts, lumpy with the strain of unreleased milk, he mumbled, "We're a little concerned about the shape of the baby's head. We're going to run some tests to see if he has hydrocephalus."

Life stopped. My heart skipped a beat; my facial muscles froze. The world narrowed, and it would never, never look the same again.

"What are you talking about? What's hydrocephalus?"

"Oh," he said casually, "it's a disease that causes the head to grow abnormally." He pulled up the sheet and headed for the door; hesitating, he groped for a comforting phrase. "Don't worry," he finally managed, "you can have more kids."

Jackie broke the cold silence. "You're worried about what he said, aren't you?"

"Yeah. What's he talking about?"

"Oh, I wouldn't worry, it didn't sound too serious." She hid her face behind a hand mirror, and didn't speak to me again. I hardly noticed when she packed up and left the hospital with her baby, but sat immobilized, thinking not of my baby's probable pain, not of the uncertain future, but of the past: the past nine months. What had I done wrong?

I had conceived under less than ideal conditions: in the back of a car, unmarried. In a panic, I married a man who was a virtual stranger to me. During my pregnancy I'd had a vaginal infection, and, not knowing what a vaginal infection was, felt too ashamed to tell the doctor. I had watched my weight rather than nutrition, starving myself prior to checkups, and was proud to gain only 16 pounds total—never mind that this was encouraged by my doctor, who'd asserted that that "eating for two is an old wives' tale"—this was now one of my wrongdoings. In my ninth month I'd gone swimming in a public pool, only to learn later that some doctors advised against this. Worst of all, I had made love beyond the allotted time limit, up until three short weeks ago.

The litany never ended. With each passing day, year, decade, new sins were added to the list. Cigarettes. Coffee. Alcohol. Aspirin. I devoured reports of new medical discoveries, acquiring ammunition against myself. Sodium pentathol: I should have had natural childbirth. Radiation in cow's milk: I should have been drinking soy milk. Zinc. Calcium. Iron pills. Every time that child cried in pain or staggered under the weight of his head, my heart would cry out *mea culpa*.

Foggily I climbed out of bed to join the other mothers walking up and down the corridors in their new E.J. Korvette bathrobes. I saw them as characters in a science fiction movie, machines that had fulfilled their baby-making function, now useless and bored. I don't know, maybe they were walking around in a state of grace, ecstasy even, but as I said, the world had narrowed.

I walked to the phone booth and began dialing Bob's office, but stopped midway, remembering his demeanor the previous night: surely he had known. He had known something was wrong with our baby and he'd deliberately kept it from me. I hung up the receiver and sat in the booth absorbing this information.

Never had I felt so betrayed. However well-intentioned were Bob's motives in withholding vital information from me, I would never fully recover from this sense of betrayal; if we'd been strangers when we'd married, we were now on our way to becoming enemies.

I picked up the phone again and called my sister.

"Linda? I just found out that the baby might have something called hydrocephalus."

"Dammit. Who told you?"

Again the bottom fell out of my world. "You mean you knew?"

"Well, Bob didn't want you to know until you'd had a chance to recover from the birth, so we all had to act like nothing was wrong."

My husband. My sister. My parents. I was surrounded by a band of lying traitors.

Stunned, I walked slowly back to my room. Bob was sitting in the armchair by my bed. He didn't notice me at first, so for a minute I was able to observe him. His neck was moving around oddly, wiggling upward as if trying to remove his head from the rest of his body; it was an involuntary tic that I'd never seen on him before, but would see often in the coming months.

Suddenly he seemed smaller than 6'4" and 200 pounds, weaker than the burly football player he was, more vulnerable than the barroom bouncer he'd been when I'd met him. My anger at him dissolved, as I realized that he too was suffering. This baby was his child also; his first child; his son—with all the weight that word carries for a man like Bob. He looked up and, seeing me, opened his big bear arms. I fell into them, sobbing.

Silently we comforted each other. Finally I said, "To tell you the truth I can't imagine this happening to anyone else we know."

"You mean we're losers?" he asked.

"Yeah," I said softly, feeling a great wave of shame flood over me. "That's what I mean."

I had, after all, failed the greatest test of womanhood—for women ultimately prove their worth by bearing healthy children. Indeed, in the recovery room Bob had whispered, "You came through with flying colors, kid." Now I'd learned that I had not, in fact, delivered flawlessly.

I had not been a rockbed of self-esteem to begin with; now I felt as if some inner deformity had manifested itself in my child, who would henceforth provide living proof of my defectiveness.

The hospital suspended normal visitation rules, allowing

Bob to stay with me all day. On and off I cried, on and off I raged. I wanted the baby to live. I wanted the baby to die. I wanted the baby not to have this disease with the evil-sounding name.

When Daryl was brought in for feeding again, I studied him with a sharper eye. I saw what I'd missed before: his head was only slightly larger than normal, but asymmetrical. Tentatively I touched it: it seemed so vulnerable, he was so vulnerable. I felt a fierce desire to protect him, and at the same time, a certain amount of fear—not fear of what might happen to him, but an inexplicable fear of him, of his strangeness.

My parents came to visit again; this time Jackie was gone, and we had the room to ourselves. My mother stood at the foot of the bed, smiling brightly, chattering inanely.

"Ma," I finally said, "You do know about the baby, don't you?"

"Know what?"

"About the hydrocephalus."

"Oh, that. So, he'll have an operation."

Her characteristic lack of emotion enraged me. "You don't care, do you?" I shouted. "You don't even care!"

Her smile never wavered, but her eyes burned like dry ice, imparting their usual message: "Get control of yourself."

I had no intention of getting control of myself: My mother had known something was wrong with my baby, and had marched in here smiling. Worse, she had somehow led me to this hospital bed with never a hint at what might transpire. A husband might betray, a father, even a sister—but a mother was not supposed to betray.

"You're like some kind of robot," I cried, leaping forward on the bed. My shouts drew the attention of a nurse.

"Visiting hours are over," she announced briskly, shooing everyone out, though there were at least another fifteen minutes to go. After she'd emptied the room, she returned with my usual vitamin pill and, beside it, a new capsule.

"What's this?" I asked.

"Just a little something to help you sleep."

Dutifully I swallowed my "medicine" and awoke the next morning not only refreshed but optimistic. Suddenly I, like my mother, felt that nothing was terribly wrong.

The pediatrician came to explain my baby's condition and probable operation. Hydrocephalus, he told me, is a disease of the central nervous system wherein cerebro-spinal fluid, rather than circulating normally, accumulates in the head, causing it to grow rapidly and exerting pressure on the brain. The word literally translates as "water on the brain," a phrase commonly used to denote stupidity in popular "jokes," a phrase that would from this day forward cause me to cringe reflexively. In the past, I learned, babies with hydrocephalus either outgrew the condition—sometimes with brain damage—or died. In the late 1950s an operation was devised wherein a plastic tube, or shunt, is inserted beneath the scalp, stretching into the chest or stomach cavity, draining the fluid. Daryl's head was only slightly larger than a normal infant's and so his prognosis was good.

Under the effect of pills, which I never suspected until years later were mood elevators, I began to view Daryl's condition as if it were no more significant than a mole or a wart.

When my obstetrician came in later, he asked if the pediatrician had been to see me.

"Oh sure," I said, waving my arm in the air. "He told me all about hydrocephalus. Did you know Winston Churchill had it and he outgrew it?"

"No, I didn't," said my doctor, frowning as he checked my breasts.

"Well, he did. But I guess Daryl's going to need an operation."

"Hm. Well, anyhow, you can have more kids."

I snapped my gum in his face, mentally willing him out of my consciousness. "Daryl is going to be fine," I said, despising him.

My grandfather called to suggest institutionalizing the baby.

"Just think," he reasoned, "you'll be stuck for the rest of your life."

"He's going to be fine, Grampa," I said, rolling my eyes at Bob, who sat beside me, as if exasperated with an old man's senility. "He just needs an operation."

A friend who'd heard something was "wrong" with my baby telephoned.

"Oh," I explained in response to the concern in Louann's voice, "he has something called hydrocephalus. They're going to do an operation and then he'll be okay."

"Thank God," she said. I could almost hear the rosary beads clicking in her devout Catholic hands. "At least it isn't a missing limb or something really bad."

"Oh, no, nothing like that. Really. He'll be fine."

Bob was astounded by my change in attitude. Beneath my bravado and drug-induced oblivion, though, I was feeling more and more isolated from the mainstream of humanity, a feeling that would intensify and affect me for the rest of my life. There were those who, like my grandfather, acted as if Daryl's birth was a dire tragedy, while others, like Louann, were relieved that he didn't have "something really bad." Both attitudes denied reality. Neither left room for me to express my feelings—a mixture of fear, shame and disappointment.

Ah, the disappointment! Sure, I'd gotten pregnant by default, but the truth was, I had wanted a baby for as long as I could remember. I adored my little cousins, and once I was respectably married, I'd been ecstatic over my pregnancy. I shopped for baby clothes with joy, appreciated the smiles of strangers as my belly grew, and devoured books on child-rearing. I thought about dressing up my baby, taking her (invariably I fantasized a her) out in her stroller, playing with dolls in our apartment. I couldn't wait to have my very own little baby, for in my limited experience, babies were playthings.

Most parents eventually learn that babies aren't playthings. I learned it in one brutal day.

Dead Brother

By Julie Geen

I played the dead brother card for years after he died. Weekdays I waited for the bus to take me from the suburban Colorado prairie, a land made emptier by the tract houses that replaced miles of waving grass, to a city school. My cruel best friend Wendy waited with me. Her David Cassidy haircut, the very best thing a person of either sex could have in 1974, and her ability to smoke at age twelve without coughing, made her my master. "All you talk about is horses, and it's boring," she told me, bringing instant tears. When she rolled her eyes and asked what was wrong I said, "I'm crying about Mikey." She narrowed her eyes, but she got quiet. It really only worked once. After that, she said, "You just want me to feel sorry for you."

We have a home movie of when he was just home from the hospital. He's a little clay infant, and my mom is trying to breathe life into him. She's animated and uses her whole body and her mouth moves, pumping him with encouraging words. He has the round, bland angel face of all Downs babies, his eyes unfocused and his body at once stiff and limp. It's fruitless, you can tell.

My father had a knack with the Super 8. His shots were well staged: He came in late and left early, like a good director should. He captured rainbows, my mom with her arms curved reverently around a lapful of kittens, Christmas trees radiating tinsel, my brother like a little owl in his bouncy seat taking it all in. And, of course, me: my first ecstatic, out of control ride on my new rocking horse, my cakes, my friends in pointed party hats. And, my mom's butt. Pretty much every time he picked up the camera he got a shot or two.

I played with my brother. We shared a room in our tiny ranch house, me in my twin bed and him in his crib. He would lie on his back and stare, and I would pretend he was my husband and cook things for him, prattling away, pumping him with my own words. He sucked up all the attention in our house. He needed all the life we had.

Two years later, right before my mother gave birth to her third child, my parents institutionalized him. I asked my mom if they gave him away because he was bad. His crib had a new, perfect baby sister in it a scant few weeks later. I was thrilled to have a sister. I had asked God for one, and my order was filled. The camera didn't come out very often. My sister goes from being a tiny scrap with enormous eyes, to crawling, to high-stepping in the grass in a bubble-shaped sun suit, in one roll of film. Maybe the camera wasn't a novelty anymore. Maybe my dad was overwhelmed. Or maybe there's a hole he didn't want to record.

We visited my brother at the institution on Sundays. There is footage of him scooting furiously across the gray industrial linoleum, and standing, triumphantly shaking the hell out of a Christmas tree, and my mom's butt as she tries to save it.

Mikey grew, but very slowly. At seven, he was like a two year old, barely walking and in diapers. He reminded me of Boris Karloff in the 1932 *Frankenstein* movie, except he was much shorter and way cuter. He walked with a staggering lurch, and was genial except when thwarted. He loved ice cream more than anything, and shoveled it in, roaring with joy until he howled in pain from a brain freeze. His other favorite thing was to take one of his shoes and dangle it from the lace and make it spin. He grinned and gave beautiful, deep, demonic chortles.

The last home movie of him shows him, handsome in a navy blue jumper, squinting and grinning at his cake with seven candles like a pirate. He has a new ball, and laughs and spins his shoe on top of it and then a golden light blooms and fills the screen, taking him over. Maybe it was the end of the film roll, or maybe it got overexposed. He came down with spinal meningitis shortly after his birthday. My father never picked up the movie camera again.

Mikey was hospitalized for two months. I spent a lot of time at a family friend's house near the hospital while my parents stayed with him. It was May, and all the kids from the neighborhood and I ran through the Colorado spring night past the blooming lilac bushes playing ring and run and catch and kiss games. I told Brandy that my parents said he might die. My little friend looked at me with her big brown eyes and told me that God would never let my brother die, and I felt happy and ran off again, even though I had a shadowed place in me that knew he would.

My grandma Jane came to stay during his last week. She insisted I sleep with her. She was scary with her violent mood swings and her pure hatred of my mother, but she smelled really good and wore frilly pink nighties and had very grown up conversations with me about all the things other adults did that were wrong and bad. So that was good.

She and I were awake and talking in the pink gold light that flooded the room at sunrise when my mom knocked on the door. I knew why.

"It's over." She sobbed. I did not know until many years later that my parents were told he was brain dead and removed him from life support the night before.

I remember my parents' bedroom door closed, and my mother's screams. My world split. Before the screams, it was relatively safe; after them, I knew that things could happen that could destroy you.

I rode to the funeral with my other grandma and her latest husband. Grandma Betty wore her dyed red hair all piled up on her head saloon girl style and walked with a swing in her hips that made Grandma Jane's nose go up in the air and her lips freeze in a small superior smile. This newest grandpa arrived to pick me up in a Cadillac with slippery leather seats, and his hair all slicked back. His big wide libertine face was softened and his loud voice composed. Dead kids bring out the best in people.

It was open casket, and my parents and I saw him before

the funeral. Mikey was laid out as if ready for a winter night in a blue blanket sleeper, with a teddy bear donated by my little sister tucked under his arm. I studied him carefully, immediately fascinated by the mortician's work. Clearly his eyes and mouth had been glued shut. And I thought his arm looked weird, like maybe it had been cut off. So, my mother had to field a few macabre questions as she said her last goodbye to her little boy. "Mama, are his eyes glued shut? Is that his real arm?" My father's body bowed over the coffin in naked sorrow and he kissed Mikey on the forehead. I admired his courage. My dead brother scared the hell out of me.

My own sorrow erupted during the service. Close family was off to the side, secluded. My sobs were raw and loud. The minister looked over at me, and I thought I saw irritation in his eyes. I was ruining my dead brother's show. After the funeral, we stood in a receiving line of sorts and Mikey's nurses and caretakers at the institution filed by, holding my parents and crying. I felt relieved to see them cry. They had loved him.

Watching my father break was bad. My father was a policeman. Sometimes he would come home from work with bloody knuckles, or once, unable to talk except in a dry rasp, with dull purple fingerprints circling his throat and a shadowed look in his eyes. But he was stronger than the darkness he battled at night. He was quiet and always alert and no matter how fast he drove, I always felt safe. Now his big shoulders shook, and his handsome strong face fell into slashes of sorrow and tears dropped as he cried silently and unexpectedly many times during the day. My mother was brittle and hard in her grief. Our Sundays gaped, lost and open. I don't remember what we did to fill them.

Sometime later that year, I won a bike at K-Mart for a drawing I did. The contest was to draw the pet you would most like to have and I drew a sorrel horse, using my burnt sienna crayon, standing at the top of a canyon. We went to K-Mart, and got to hear them announce it over the loudspeaker, and describe my drawing to all the shoppers. My bike was green. My parents were proud, but I could see they had to work at it. Everything they said, and all the motions of their daily life were layered over a grief that flattened everything. I rode the bike I won for the first time, and it felt good, but not that good. I had the flatness in me, too. My parents divorced a few years later.

As my own son approached his seventh birthday, some thirty-six years after Mikey's death, fear threaded through me. My rational mind scoffed, my deeper mind whispered that seven was not a good number for a little boy. The first time my father came to visit after my boy had sprouted his downy blond hair, he held my son in his lap and his hand trembled and his voice shook as he stroked his head. "His hair is the same." I didn't have to ask whose he meant.

Anxiety is part of my weave, sometimes taunt and binding, sometimes faded like a background color. My whole family assumes there has been a car wreck, quietly, to themselves, if someone is late. If one of her grandchildren germinates a fever in her vicinity, my mother has hysteria in her voice that makes my sister and I seize up. We feign elaborate casualness in our parenting. But we know we are not safe. We know that forces beyond our control can reach into a family and pluck out a child.

Crossroads

By Cara Bruce

The car disappeared. Careening speedily in front of us, it ducked around turns on the serpentine road, its back lights appearing and disappearing like a winking eye.

We slid around another turn, our wheels hugging the pavement, our bodies waving with centrifugal force; we looked up, and it was gone. And for that breath there was nothing but blackness, the thin outline of the empty road unrolling beneath our wheels.

We slowed down. We had been driving fast but not nearly as fast as the car in front of us, a beat up old hatchback, whose scratched sides held five of our friends. The thick trees that grew up on either side of that thin road morphed from blurred browns and greens into more definitive outlines; a smudged charcoal painting coming into focus. Our world was dark, no streetlights, no moon, and those thick trees blocked out even the largest star.

Birdsfoot Road. One of those curvy, country back roads.

A road drawn by an epileptic or perhaps a child, a road that twisted and turned, unreasonably following the natural curve of the land, like an eroding river. A road with no stop signs, no reflectors, nothing except the fluttering window lights shining back through the woods, the promise of deeply nestled houses, their owners tucked snugly inside, unaware of the tragedy unfolding before them.

"There." Dana, my best friend who was driving, pointed to her left, a slight hill rolled into more woods, and there, at the bottom, the elusive lights. We pulled over; there was no curb, no sidewalk, just road and then dirt, hard and then soft. We stepped carefully out of the car, aware that something was wrong, afraid of the spectral stories our minds were already spinning. The air hung limp with leftover humidity. Virginia summers always dripped wet. In the daytime you could walk outside and the heat would hit you right between the eyes, physically, like a punch. The night was cooler, a time of relief, still hot but not always so painful. The type of weather that makes you tired, that makes walking difficult, the air heavy as a forgotten swamp. Yet night was when we woke up; when we were free. We could run, we could play, limbs moved without effort, shackles discarded. What a difference in degrees.

Standing at the top of the hill felt like a scene from a movie: the car had landed right side up at the bottom, its headlights shone into the darkness, illuminating the woods, and the music, some Oi! hardcore, still blasting its awful soundtrack, the frenzy of the music making the moment even more surreal, more macabre. Most of our friends were walking up the hillside. One body had been thrown out of the car and lay discarded on the grass. It was Mason, the driver. It sounded like he was moaning and it took me a moment to realize that he was simply trying to breathe. It was horrible—each inhalation and exhalation equally pained and raspy, so much that it made my own chest hurt. As we continued down the others walked up, limping, disoriented, patting their heads and chests to make sure they were still intact. Out of the three of them there was a broken leg, a bruised head, a pained shoulder, but they were breathing normally. They were alive.

Yet, one was missing.

We reached the bottom of the car. He sat in the back seat, as if he had simply chosen not to get out, or possibly even dozed off. His head drooped forward and something trickled from his mouth.

It was the first time I saw a dead body. I was fifteen, and he was my friend.

There are moments in your life when everything changes. For the majority of my life I haven't realized they were occurring. I didn't notice that something important was happening until I looked back, contemplated, and said: *Oh yeah,* that's *when my life turned.* Crossroads moments: moments when I made a choice that had a substantial effect on the later course of my life. However, *this* was a moment of impact, a moment when I knew what was happening, when I was fully aware of a major and lasting change occurring in my consciousness.

One of my friends, someone that I cared about, was dead. He was only a few years older than me and he lived in a town house with my boyfriend and another friend. I had a group of friends and there were groups within that larger group, we may have teased each other, made fun of each other, but we cared about one another. We were, in a way, an extended family. Of course some of us didn't truly *like* each other, while others paired off, bonded, and became close. But everyone loved Curtis. In a word, he was kind.

He had been sitting in the back seat of the car, in the middle, between two of our friends. The other people in the car told us that before they crashed he had turned to each of the boys sitting next to him, kissed them on the mouth, and said good-bye. Did he know that he was going to die? Did he feel something? See something? Did his too short life flash in front of his closing eyes?

Curtis had plans, dreams, he was going to fully live his life, he may have even made a difference; he was that kind of guy. But he didn't. Instead, on a summer's night, on a dark road, on the way to a party, in the back seat of a car, his neck snapped… and he was gone.

And it was another one of my friends who killed him.

Mason had been drinking. We didn't see him drink but we all knew that he was drunk. He was driving fast, erratically, more so than usual. I'm sure that he didn't consider the lives he held in his hands. I fully believe that nothing was intentional. We were going to a party, eight of us, in two cars. I never knew whose party it was, or where they lived. I still don't. It was just one more destination where I would never arrive.

Mason was flown away by helicopter. They saved his life, yet neglected to test his blood alcohol level.

There was an open casket. If I hadn't known it was Curtis, I would never have recognized him. His face was swollen. He looked made of putty, made of play-doh. Sometimes when I close my eyes I still see him like that, so damn heavy.

Months after the accident we went to court. We were called to testify about what happened, but, like I said, none of us had seen him drinking. He never came into the house. And until he was thrown from the car onto that darkened hillside, he never left it. For two days we sat in that anonymous courthouse, waiting in a secluded room with industrial carpet and fake wooden furniture, until we were called one by one to share our stories.

Maybe we were lucky that we didn't know anything: that we weren't forced to choose between friends, to testify. In a way, we were granted a reprieve. Because we knew he was drunk, there was no question in any of our minds, yet we had not physically witnessed it. The other thing we knew, without question, was that it could have happened to any of us. We may not have said the words out loud but in our minds, in our hearts, we knew it to be true. All of us had gotten into a car with a friend who was drunk. And most of us, those with driver's licenses, had driven under the influence at one time or another. Any one of us could have been the victim. Or the killer.

Mason walked away with a slap on the wrist, a $25 fine, something that must have tasted sour, like a spoiled joke, to Curtis's mother. I can only imagine that it was insult upon the gravest of injuries. Back then things were much more black and white, my world hadn't yet turned its ambivalent and ambiguous shade of grey.

I often think back on those moments: my breath catching

in my throat when I saw that car idling at the bottom of the hill, peering in at Curtis's dead body, and later, when I finally realized that Mason wasn't the enemy, he was merely the wrong drunk teenager behind the wrong wheel at the wrong time. But what truly shaped me was the moment I realized things weren't so cut and dry, that any of us could be the bad guy and any of us could be that lone passenger left behind.

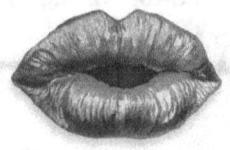

Crooked

By Amy Yelin

The first time it happens I am 11 years old and in the family den, nestled among brown paneling, the familiar voice of Allen Funt coming from the Zenith, and the smell of my favorite TV dinner—chicken with mashed potatoes, peas, and cranberry cobbler for dessert—in the air. Although I don't recall a trigger for the attack, death is the theme, the idea being that my parents will die; that I will die. When it strikes, the world goes wavy, as though someone has knocked my antennae over; as though I am suddenly drowning in air. Frightened, I bury my head like an ostrich in my mother's orange swivel corduroy chair.

"What the heck are you doing?" My sister Jackie asks, walking in the room and slapping me on the butt.

"Nothing," I say, my voice muffled by the chair.

"Turn around then."

I turn around and sit normally. Thankfully, the world steadies again.

"Your face looks funny," Jackie says while running one finger down her cheek.

I touch my face and feel indents in my skin, remnants from the corduroy.

Jackie sits down in the middle of the room, directly in front of the TV.

"You're going to die," I tell her, hoping she might convince me otherwise.

"Whatever," she says. "Where's the kvetch?"

I reach under a pillow and throw her the remote control.

"Aren't you afraid of dying?" I ask her.

"Nope," she says. Then she sucks her thumb, a longstanding habit—she is now 14—that makes her right thumb look permanently deformed and waterlogged. With the other hand, she twirls some strands of her dirty blond hair.

We watch *Candid Camera* and, for the moment, forget about death.

A few weeks later, Jackie is diagnosed with scoliosis. Like her thumb, her spine is also deformed and she will need an operation to fix it. My father explains that a surgeon will remove the crooked piece of her back and replace it with a metal rod. The worst part is the cast she will have to wear for five months after surgery, which my father describes as extending from her hips to just under her chin, encasing my sister like a human turtle.

I feel bad for her. As sisters go, we are close. We play jacks and board games together, classics like *Monopoly*, *Operation*, and *Life*, my favorite. There's something about the simplicity and straightforwardness of the game of *Life*: stay on the road, get married, have children, win money, and retire. Not to mention doing it all in a little convertible. I think how wonderful it will be to grow up.

Many nights, after we finish our games, I pull the mattress from the cot into Jackie's room and sleep on her floor. Sometimes we watch *Soap* or *Charlie's Angels* on her little black-and-white TV. Other nights we talk Pig Latin to each other: "Ellohay ackieJay!" Then laugh.

Occasionally she lets me sleep in her bed, mostly when it's stormy outside. In matching candy-cane-striped foot pajamas, we spoon. She whispers in my ear that the thunder is just God bowling upstairs; the lighting a sign he's scored a strike.

While she is in the hospital, my parents give me a key and let me stay home alone after school for the first time. I don't like it.

"Can I go with you today?" I ask them each morning. But the answer is always no.

"You won't like the hospital anyway," my mother says, "trust me."

It isn't until a few days after Jackie's surgery—which coincides with the start of Passover—that they are forced to take me with them. We will be visiting my sister before going to my grandparents' apartment on the Lower East Side for the annual Seder. I get my way, but it is thanks to Moses, my father jokes, and not my powers of persuasion.

My parents are right: I do not like the hospital. The floor that my sister is on is dimly lit and bare. Shouldn't it be nicer, I wonder, brighter... to cheer up the patients? I grip my mother's hand tightly as we walk toward Jackie's room.

When we enter, Jackie is propped up in her bed, the top of her new body cast spouting forth from the opening of her hospital gown. Her TV is on. The moment she sees us walk in, she starts to cry.

"I want to take this off," she says, "please take it off."

While my parents try to console her, I stand against a wall and keep my eyes on the television. Gilligan has been hit on the head by a coconut and has lost his memory.

"*Please*," Jackie begs. "I'm itchy..." My father leaves and finds a nurse, a stern lady who explains that itching is common, and who demonstrates how to pour cornstarch down the cast.

In the car, my parents say little. I feel relieved to be out of the hospital but then, before we are even out of the parking garage, it happens again. The world goes wavy and I start to drown, this time to the soundtrack of Kansas's "Dust in the Wind" on the car radio. I bury my face in the vinyl backseat until the feeling passes.

We arrive late for the Seder at my grandparents' apartment. My parents take the old-fashioned elevator while I take the stairs four flights; the first symptom of what will become a lifelong phobia.

"Hello Boobeee!" my Aunt Helen says as she opens the door. She kisses me half-lipped while the other half skillfully balances one long Virginia Slim. I cringe. It is the same with my Uncle Harvey. Between hacking coughs and with a smashed stub still burning in the ashtray, they each light up another, until cigarettes seem like extra appendages hanging off their lips.

While my aunt calls me "Boobeee," my grandmother calls me "Bubala" or "Amyla." Although I am polite—I have stopped hiding under furniture when my grandparents come to visit—I still do not like to be close to them. I have an aversion to old age; even the Santa Claus at the local shopping center makes me uncomfortable. To me, the elderly are more like creepy extraterrestrials rather than something I too will become one day.

For the Seder, we sit at a table in the living room arranged specifically for the holiday. It is placed in the only area where it will fit in the apartment, between the green plastic-covered chairs on one side, and the green plastic-covered couch on the other. Unlike our house in the suburbs, my grandparents' apartment is small. It has an old-fashioned kitchen, a living room and two bedrooms. My grandparents sleep in one bedroom in separate twin beds. In the other room, the room where my mother and her two sisters grew up (an amazing feat, I think, the three of them in one room together) there is one queen-size bed. This is where my parents and I will be spending the night.

The moment we sit down at the Seder table, my grandfather begins reciting from the Seder book. He does this the way he communicates most things that involve religion or politics, with volume and passion. As he spews off the words in Hebrew that I don't understand, gobs of white spit fly from the corners of his mouth and his yarmulke gradually slips from his white head and lands in his plate. He doesn't seem to notice. Hiding a yawn, I lean the pages of the Seder booklet against my face and inhale the smell of paper. My stomach growls; I glance at the food on the table. There isn't much to choose from: some horseradish, something that resembles leaves, matzo, and hard-boiled eggs.

"They're symbolic." My mother once explained to me when I complained about the choices.

My grandfather's spit flies again and lands on one of the hardboiled eggs. I laugh, and my cousins, like dominoes, follow suit. This causes him to slam a fist on the table and raise the volume, his voice booming now as though it is actually the voice of Moses himself.

My father, on the other hand, does Passover differently. When it is his turn, he also reads in Hebrew, but his voice is quieter, less passionate. When we giggle again, for some other childish reason, he does not raise his voice, or bang a fist. He simply keeps going. When he finishes, he looks relieved. He flashes me a playful wink.

That night, a short time after the Seder is complete, my grandfather gets sick. "Too much Manischewitz wine," Uncle Harvey declares, the appendage jiggling from his lip with each word.

My grandfather has his head stuck out the living room window as he vomits. I imagine it's a combination of matzo, hardboiled eggs and macaroons. It scares me, the way he pushes his head out so far, the way the window frame is bobbing up and down on his neck. My father tries to pull him back inside, but he won't budge. My grandmother exchanges worried glances with her two daughters, but no one is speaking. Above the faint retching sounds coming from my grandfather, all you can hear is the sound of plastic crinkling, people shifting nervously in their seats.

Later, wedged between my parents, it is impossible to sleep. I keep picturing my sister in her hospital bed, sealed inside her cast, unable to turn over, unable to scratch. And then, there is my grandfather. He is in the bathroom most of the night, right outside our bedroom door. I can see the yellow glow of the bathroom light, his shadow in the hallway. I can hear him throwing up in the toilet. I cover my ears and anxiously wait for morning.

***

By the end of that summer, things change. My sister, like a snake shedding its skin, is freed from her cast, revealing a scarred but now perfectly aligned back. No doubt she carries other scars, but it is difficult to tell if her anger and distance are part of being a teenager, or something else.

I am different too, having recently mastered one of the essential womanly arts: shaving my legs, courtesy of my counselor at sleep away camp. There is more, although my parents' letters all summer—which provide the standard stick of gum and the note "Buddy says hi"—reveal nothing.

It is my father who finally tells me the news in a rare father-daughter moment that begins when I am shaving my legs in my parents' bathroom. I have been home from camp for two days.

"Look!" I say to my father, who is leaning in the bathroom doorway. I show him how I dip the razor in water to clean it off, and then pull it in a straight line up my cream-covered calf to remove the hair.

"Very impressive," he says and smiles. "Just don't cut yourself."

I laugh. "Now why would I do that?"

He smiles. "When you're done, come and talk to me. I have something to tell you."

I finish in a hurry, only one leg complete, my curiosity piqued. I find my father in typical fashion, resting on his side of my parents' king size bed, a book in hand with the low hum of an oldies radio station in the background.

I sit down next to him. "What did you want to tell me?"

He stops reading. He is silent for a minute or two, struggling to find the words, before finally saying, "Your grandfather died." He is talking to me, but his eyes are gazing toward the window.

"What happened?" I ask. "When?" I am surprised to feel tears running down my cheeks.

"In August," my father says. "He had a stroke in July. He never got better."

My father pauses and, with a flicker of uncertainty, adds, "We didn't want to ruin your summer."

He gently rubs my arm and for a moment, I am angry. The man giving me comfort is also the man who kept a secret from me. I start to push my father away but then bury my face in his shoulder, into the familiar smell of Aqua Velva cologne. To my relief, the world does not go wavy again. In fact it won't for another 13 years. Yet, at that moment, I still feel disoriented, like the way one feels when stumbling into unfamiliar territory.

It's as though without my wanting to I have turned down a road where life gets messier: A road where grandparents die and beloved fathers keep secrets and sisters, once carefree and loving, grow rigid and cold. It's a road, I sense sadly, from which there is no going back.

Baptism

By Joy Wilson-Young

When the phone rang early on the morning of July 19, 1985, Grandma, who hardly slept because of back and leg pain, was already awake and finishing off a pack of Pall Malls. She rose from the kitchen table, slowly walking to the black rotary phone. As she listened she nodded and somewhere near the end of the conversation she said, "I knew that man was a sorry son of a bitch." I got dressed. The sleepover was finished; we packed my Snoopy suitcase, put Brandy, Grandma's Sheltie, into the back seat of her Cadillac and she drove me home. We walked into my house in time to see my father on the television: a picture I now know as his mug shot. He was wearing his thick glasses, but instead of his work shirt, he wore a white jumpsuit. According to the broadcast, he'd been "arrested on a number of charges."

Mom was sitting at the dining room table. Her glasses were in her hand and she stared at the television, her eyes red and puffy, her shirt wet from wiping them. When she noticed me with my suitcase she started bawling and Grandma said, "Joyce, you go on outside to play with the dog. Check on the girls, Angel. And take Brandy with you."

My sisters, Deidre and April, were sitting in the swings out back. The three of us were quiet with the knowledge that something terrible had happened.

On the afternoon my family found out my father was arrested for rape and burglary, a group of thin Brothers and their over-stuffed wives from our LDS Church Ward convened in our living room. They looked at us with a mixture of pity and doubt, as if we were co-conspirators. Mom got down on her knees while one of the Brothers held his hand on her head and prayed. Then he sprinkled water onto her from a metal vial around his neck. Mom cried the way only a woman whose husband had been keeping secrets could cry—tears of shame and ignorance.

Grandma smoked one cigarette after the other in the front yard and snubbed them out into the marigolds Mom had just planted.

The thin Brothers moved onto praying over us while their wives set up shop in our kitchen. While the holy water ran down my forehead and caught in my eyelashes, I could feel them staring. We were the Wilson women, women who let my father's evil into our house.

Today I've taken a trip to the Salvation Army and have found a gem—a huge mirror that used to be part of a bedroom suite, but is now bereft of its dresser. It's too heavy to lift and I hadn't grabbed a buggy when I walked in. Afraid of losing my find to an elderly woman in black Keds who seemed to be watching my every move, I hang onto the mirror like an anchor and drag it toward my husband, Adam. He's found the books, so we may be here another half-hour.

I'm perusing the Salvation Army's intake of writing guides—an old Funk and Wagnalls, a Strunk and White with pages torn out, a 2005 *Writer's Market*. It's then that I spot, out of the corner of my eye, the Keds-clad elderly woman. She's coming toward me and I just know she's going to make a point of asking me to get out of her way as she has two previous times this afternoon. She stops shy of me by three feet, and I think for a moment she's going to insist I hand over the mirror. She says, "What in the world is God doing? I'll-tell-you-what-he's-doing-he's-being-our-personal-savior-if-we-let-him-Amen." Then she walks on.

My mouth is dry; I don't know what to do. Should I say something as she goes?

Instead I look up and stare at Adam; sure he's heard her remark. But he's got his back to me and is deep into a blurb for a Western. I glance around. No one else is within earshot. Before I can ask her why she's asking me this question, she's high-tailing it toward the cashier as fast as her Keds can carry her.

I'm sure Adam is just being polite not to laugh until she's out of earshot, so I begin to lug the heavy mirror in his direction. I pass through the aisle the way the elderly woman has come. There, sitting on a rack marked Religious, is a book with the title *What in the World is God Doing?*

I wait until we've loaded the mirror into the car and are on our way for a fast food lunch treat before I blurt out the entire story. Adam's laughing over the ordeal, telling me a story about a friend of his mother's who ended every sentence with Amen. "Pass the cornbread, Amen," he's saying. "Boy this sure is a nice car, Amen." He's laughing so hard he doesn't see that we should move ahead in the drive-thru.

I fail to see the humor in this situation. I'm sure the elderly woman singled me out for a few reasons. First, and most obvious, the huge mirror I snagged for fifteen dollars; hers was a question not about God's general intentions but about why he'd allowed me to find the mirror before she could. Second, and slightly less obvious, was the fact that she had to ask me twice to get out of her way as I tugged the mirror up and down the aisles; God did not like impolite twenty-something's who hogged aisle space in crowded discount stores. Last, obvious only to me because I instantly assume looks are everything, (and because, in the summer, when I'm working in the garden and writing, I wear the same clothes for days on end and find no reason to bathe), I tell Adam, "It's because I look homeless or something. I've got no make-up on, dirty jeans, and I stink. She thought I might need some help from her god. Or at least the god on the book cover. I really need a shower."

"What did she have on, Amen?" Adam laughs.

"Keds. Black ones. A really nice silk blouse like my grandma used to wear, belted at the waist."

He says, "That's a really nice belt you've got there," and busts up laughing again before he adds, "Amen."

"Cut it out."

"Okay, Amen."

When I began dating Adam, the younger of two sons raised in a Southern Baptist household, I had no idea his mother was so akin to the Brothers and Sisters of the LDS church I came to resent in my childhood. She is the type of woman who prays over a kitchen fire before dousing it with baking soda; the same type of woman like those wives who were, initially, overly—offensively—sympathetic because of my father's arrest; the same type of mother like those who sat next to me at church and looked down their noses when I joined their children in singing "Jesus Wants Me for a Sunbeam." I remember their sharp eyes, their accusatory looks. They were the same eyes my soon-to-be mother-in-law fixed on me one afternoon in her home while Adam and his father grilled steaks outside. We were sitting in her living room, watching HGTV and reading *Southern Living* when she turned to me and asked, "Have you found Jesus Christ?"

For a split second I was tempted to be a smart ass and say, "I didn't know he was missing." But I didn't say this, not in that pristine Christian living room, bible verses painted onto the walls—"As for me and my house, we will serve the Lord." Instead I cleared my throat to answer but she went on, "Because He is our God. Our savior."

I crossed and re-crossed my legs. The way she said *our* made me more uncomfortable than the question itself. Surely she didn't mean Adam—my agnostic fiancé who'd been sleeping with me for the last year. Someone she raised to despise and pity lost souls like my own.

On the way back to my apartment that afternoon I told Adam what happened. He asked me to repeat the story twice and wanted to know my response. "I don't know what I said," I told him. "Words came out. I told her I'd been baptized. She never quit looking me in the eye, like I was lying. It was freaky. I wanted to tell her I don't believe in Jesus as the son of God unless it's in an Aeneas-as-the-son-of-Venus way."

"Why didn't you?"

"Have you ever told your mother you don't believe in Jesus?"

"I don't have a reason to."

"The next time we're at their house, I'll have her ask you about him. You used to be the authority on this, right?" He checked the rearview several times and adjusted the mirror. We didn't talk about it again but I couldn't get it out of my head. What about me—my curly hair, my ripped jeans, my painted toenails—made his mother assume I didn't know who Jesus Christ was? Was it because I'm from California—worse, Los Angeles County, home of homosexuals and single-mothers? And what made her think she could save my soul? I might not attend church, but I know that soul saving is reserved for the seeker and their god. Who did she think she was?

Three months after my father was arrested, I was baptized into the Church of Latter Day Saints. Because he had been, by that fall, charged with over a dozen crimes, the cleansing of my soul and my acceptance of faith were crucial. Already the stares and whispers followed me wherever I went. I spent time hiding away in my room reading books or watching from my window as the other kids on my street played with each other. If I'd joined them, they would've scattered like marbles. The same way they avoided me in school.

That night I wore my white and black checked dress and the black headband Grandma was so fond of, the one with a huge plastic red rose attached to the top that looked like a tumor. I just knew that after Brother Buzby dunked me under I was going to be a Sunbeam for Jesus.

"All you have to do is when you hear the word 'accept' is say 'yes,'" Mom said. She'd belted my two sisters into the backseat of our silver Ford sedan, and I was sitting in the front with my beach towel on my lap. "Remember," she said again, "when he asks if you accept Jesus Christ as your savior, just say 'yes' loud enough so everyone can hear you then he'll put you under the water. Blow air out of your nose like you do when you're swimming. Then you're done."

I'm not sure if my father ever knew I was baptized. That November, Mom was tight-lipped about him except to say, "He's not coming home again. Ever. He was pretending to be a good father and husband."

Grandma would say, "He's a son of a bitch jailbird. Nothing but trash."

Inside the Baptismal were folding chairs where all the witnesses would sit. Grandma was there, and Aunt Sheila and Uncle Tony, and Heather and Nick. Heather was so prissy then in her pink skirt and baby-pumps and eye shadow even though she was only nine and too young for any of it. But Grandma thought it was acceptable because Heather had just been diagnosed with diabetes and Grandma didn't think she would live to see thirty.

The Sisters had brought food. Grandma whispered,

"Mormon casserole. Yick."

"You're Mormon, Mother. Remember?" Mom said.

"I used to be Presbyterian. And before that Baptist. What's your point, Mickey?"

One of the husbands who stood watch over a platter of ham rolls was among the group who'd sprinkled Mom with holy water.

When I came out of the dressing room in my white jumpsuit everyone was seated and silent. The thin Brothers and their wives were sitting with their bibles in their laps, children seated around them. I could feel their eyes on me as I took my seat next to Deidre. Aunt Sheila and her clan were sitting in the row behind us. Deidre giggled and said, "Don't pee in there like we're in Aunt Sheila's pool." Then she snorted and I started to laugh, but Grandma looked at us like she was going to knock our teeth out.

In the fall of my second year as a professor, a very bright young man lingered after my Introduction to Composition class had ended. I assumed he wanted to talk to me about his latest essay. He'd earned a B- on the piece. I braced myself for the whining that I just knew was coming and tried to remember, exactly, how many grammar mistakes he'd made.

"Professor, can I ask you a personal question?" he began. The "personal" tactic. I'd faced it before, usually when a student knew they had no grammatical legs to stand on so they wanted to attack what they felt was my adverse reaction to their topic.

"Usually I don't answer those," I said, "but let me hear it

first."

"Do you believe in God?"

I was closing up my books and must have hesitated because he quickly went on. "Because, well, you have that Darwin pin on your bag and I just thought that maybe you didn't because, well, you have it. Right there. On your bag."

He was pointing to the button I've kept pinned to my writing bag since graduate school, something I almost never think about. Next to my Darwin fish-with-feet, is a pink Breast Cancer Awareness pin and a Happy Bunny button which reads, "Have a nice day you worthless turd." On the zipper is a bottle opener key ring that came in handy after lectures during graduate school. I couldn't help but wonder why this student wasn't asking me if I was an alcoholic, or had breast cancer, or if I thought he was a worthless turd. Which was, actually, what I was beginning to think.

I've been baited like this by students before, especially since I'm from California and I teach in rural Georgia. I'm seen as somewhat of an outsider, something to be put behind glass and mislabeled *"Atheist,* from the genus *Los Angeles, Californium."* I think my students would feel better about me if they could simply place me into one religious camp or another. Adam has to remind me after one of these moments that Christianity cannot be separated from any other aspect of life in the south.

I took a deep breath and fingered the black and white Darwin button. Then, diplomatically, I said to this bright young man whom I wanted to call a worthless turd, "I don't see how God and Darwin are mutually exclusive. There are scientists who believe in creation and evolution."

He seemed pleased with my response. "I know it was none of my business," he said. "It's just sometimes I want to talk to people about Jesus and I don't know who to ask."

It was clear he wanted me to engage him in a theological discussion, and I was flattered. But what could I say to this student who only reminded me of the thin Brothers of the LDS church? Perhaps *Sorry, you've come to the wrong person*. Or maybe something a little more personal, more direct, like, *We'd be here all night discussing my fucked-up views of how religion is a big letdown*. I'm sure he'd like to hear *You've come to the right place, my son, this way to my confessional,* but I'm not a priest or therapist. I had two more classes to teach.

I kept my trap shut and waited until he left the room before flipping him the bird. If I asked a student the question he asked me, I'd be fired. But for him to pin me into a corner is just his Christian duty. The following semester I couldn't help but notice that he didn't sign up for my Intermediate Composition course. Instead, he chose a colleague of mine, a known patron of the Methodist church. This I took as a sign of his concession of defeat.

While waiting to be baptized into the Littlerock Ward of the LDS Church, I found oddities in the people sitting around me. Grandma held her purse in her lap instead of putting it on the floor under her chair like all the Sisters. She was chewing gum and I knew the second I got out of the font she'd be in the parking lot smoking a cigarette. Nick was picking his nose. As Brother Buzby got up to address the group from the podium,

Aunt Sheila leaned over and whispered in Mom's ear, "It's a good thing you had this planned, things the way they are with Terry now." I thought of the movie *The Swiss Family Robinson*. I felt like they must've felt on their island—not dead, not alive, just lost.

Buzby was dressed in a white jumpsuit just like me. "Brothers and Sisters," he said, "today we have Joyce Elaine Wilson, daughter of Mickey Wilson and," he coughed and cleared his throat, "granddaughter of LaVerne Duval." Grandma up straight. But Buzby's words only made it more obvious that he'd excluded my father's name. "She has come before us this day to make a commitment to God. I have been chosen to conduct this service and have the honor of baptizing her. If you could all turn to Exodus, chapter twenty." The silence in the crowd was broken for a moment with the dozens of thumps and whirs of bibles opening and then Buzby went on. "This is a simple message really 'And God spoke all these words—"I am the Lord your God, who brought you out of Egypt, out of the land of slavery. You shall have no other gods before me. You should not make for yourself an idol in the form of anything in heaven above or on the earth beneath or in the waters below.""" As he droned on and on, spittle landed on the podium.

Then Buzby said the words that still chill me when I think about them: "—for I, the Lord your God, am a jealous god, punishing the children for the sin of the fathers—"

The room began to grow dark. I was passing out. I thought for the first, but not the only time in my life that Buzby was right — I was being punished for my father's sins. I was sick from it, I would be sick with it forever no matter how many times I tried to cleanse my soul or become a Sunbeam for Jesus. I sat there for a long time trying not to puke and wishing that I'd never had a father, that I'd never been born. That way, no one would ever look at me in shame again.

When Buzby finally led me down the white stairs and into the water, I could hardly walk straight. He turned me and brought my wrists together, then raised his right hand and said, "The Savior said, 'Except a man be born of water and of the spirit he cannot enter into the kingdom of God.' Do you, Joyce Elaine Wilson, accept the covenants of this church and teachings of our Lord and Savior, Jesus Christ?"

The next thing I knew I was underwater, my eyes wide open. But instead of opening my heart, letting God and Jesus and the Holy Spirit fill me up, I wished God would erase the shame that my father had caused. I wished for God to make me wise and kind, to make me someone who would never judge a person by their parents or by the way they looked. I wished to be a person who never hurt someone else. I wished for there to be a God who would only leave good things in my life so that the next time I went anywhere, people wouldn't turn away. I wished to be someone who the Brothers and Sisters wouldn't assume was as guilty as my father. Although I couldn't articulate it at the age of eight, what I was wishing for in the fall of 1985 was normalcy. But when I came up for air, the Brothers and Sisters, my aunt and cousins, my grandmother and all of the other Sunbeams were looking at me in the same way.

A Portrait of a Family
By Angela M. Graziano

December 2008

My sister, Valerie, walks in front of me. She wears a black ankle-length fake fur coat. Her hair, which, presumably, has not been washed in weeks, is slicked back into a bun—her signature style as of late. At thirty-four, her body is still small, like that of a teenage girl. She is all of 5'2", and, I imagine, does not weigh more than 110 pounds. Even her head is tiny, propped like a small, white cherry atop a giant sundae of faux fur.

I watch Valerie and my father as they hustle together, side by side, across Sixth Avenue, their lips in constant movement. This is the most I've seen them communicate in years. Or rather, it is the most I've seen them *speak* to one another in years. Lately, the bulk of their conversation has consisted of violent screaming matches. My sister, her voice masked in liquor, howling at our father about how much she hates him and wishes he were dead. Our father—the same man who, at twenty-two, married our mother and adopted my sister after her biological father abandoned them—screaming at Valerie about the mess her life has become. She had it all at thirty—a home, flashy clothes, a successful business. At thirty-four, she has nothing except for a beer belly, a police record, a storage space and a repossessed car.

Today, however, there is no screaming. Today, my father and Valerie wildly gesticulate, throwing their arms in the air and to their sides as they laugh together and share stories that are out of my hearing distance. Occasionally, my father wraps his arm around Valerie's shoulder and pulls her in close to his chest; which is when it occurs to me that this is the first time in years that they have had anything in common to talk about: their addictions.

December 1999

When I picture my father, I picture the face of Jesus.

I began to imagine my father in this way when I was a child, after I viewed a particular photograph of him. No longer do I remember how young I was when I first saw the photo; only that I was young enough to believe that my father was indeed the son of Christ.

The day I discovered the photograph went something like this: My mother and I sat on the living room carpet to sort through old photo albums. It was the first time I flipped backward through my life, thumbing through pages that marked my first Holy Communion, my first day of school, my baptism, my birth. In time, the pages permitted my entrance into a place I had never experienced or seen documented—a life before my existence. There were photographs of my parents' wedding, photographs from their bachelor days, photographs from moments before I was even a thought, let alone alive. Toward the back of the album, though, the pictures stopped and were replaced with newspaper clippings. I skimmed them and noticed my father's picture beside each chunk of text. My mother observed the inquisitive look in my eyes.

"Those are from when your father had his accident," she said and turned the page.

My father and his college girlfriend, Candy, had been traveling home to New Jersey from the Florida university they attended together when their car became sandwiched between two tractor trailers. The accident left Candy dead, three-quarters of my father's body scarred by third degree burns, and the car masked in a hellish ball of flames.

Toward the end of the photo album, I saw it: an image of my father, in his early twenties, shortly after he had returned from the physical rehabilitation center where he was learning to walk and use his newly deformed body again. It was just months before he met my mother, a young divorcée, and her seven-year old daughter, Valerie. In the picture, my father's hair was long and shaggy and he had a full, thick beard that covered his face. Something about the photo—the look of sincere mental and physical pain expressed in my father's eyes or the full, brown beard—reminded me of an image of Jesus I once saw in a children's bible.

And in that moment, I began to believe that my father, in some way, either was or held a sacred relationship with Christ.

December 2008

Walking at my side is my mother, who, to passersby, probably looks like any other mother who is joyous from the festive sights that surround her: the giant red balls perched in front of my former office in the Time Warner building (a fact that brings her great pride); the wicker angels that line the walkways of Rockefeller Square; the massive evergreen tree, standing tall among the city's buildings, its branches sparkling with layers of light. But I know none of these things are what bring a smile to my mother's face. Rather, she smiles at the simplicity of the moment: one daughter walks at her side while one daughter walks just feet from her. I know the way my mother thinks. She is a simple woman. She does not care about expensive jewelry. She has never traveled any place deemed exotic. The only thing in this world that matters to her is her family which is exactly why these last few years have been so hard on her. Not knowing where one of her children is located. Not knowing if she is safe. Phone numbers of detox centers and rehab centers and police stations in every town in our county saved to her speed dial. I see my mother's chest rise and fall in a smooth motion beneath her heavy winter coat. In this moment, she is at peace. Because she can physically see both of her daughters, she knows that, at least in these moments that we walk together, her family is safe, which, to her, means she is safe, too. The glow on her face comes from deep inside.

***

"Wake up," my mother says and gently shakes my arm. I am seventeen years old and asleep in my bed, still drunk from the delights of Christmas.

"You need to wake up, Angela," my mother says, and shakes me more firmly.

I open my eyes and see her face just inches from mine. Her skin is pale, but not a normal winter pale; more the pale of a woman who is ill. Her rounded face now indents in the centers of her cheeks; her neck is gaunter than it has ever been.

"You need to pack up your things," she says as I begin to sit upright in my bed. "We need to go and stay with your aunt up north for a while."

But I'm just a kid—just a stupid, self-consumed kid, too caught up in high school life than real life; too caught up to fully register the seriousness of my mother's tone; too self-absorbed to make sense of her sick appearance and the heaviness that has begun to consume the air of our home.

I translate her words to mean that I will be taking a short vacation to my relative's house, an hour and a half north from here, in a much more elite part of New Jersey. A treat for New Year's Eve. A reward.

My mother makes her way toward my door and then turns back to me.

"You have an hour," she says.

But the teenage prick that I am, I ignore my mother and her visible exhaustion. I leave the house and meet my boyfriend at a pizza shop on the other end of town.

My boyfriend and I sit across from one another in a vinyl booth, noshing on garlic knots and describing the clothes and CDs we received as Christmas presents—all the gifts that seem so vital now, but within just weeks, we will forget about completely. My pager rests on the table. Its screen begins to flash my home phone number alongside the numbers 911, which, in beeper code, as most other codes, means emergency.

"I think I'm going to head home," I say, kissing my boyfriend on the forehead and exiting the pizzeria.

If I had known that, in that moment, I would be exiting my childhood, too, I might have orchestrated something more memorable—a choreographed dance in the parking lot, fireworks, something. But that's the thing about life: you never know you are in the height of the most significant moments when you are actually in the process of living through them.

***

Snow falls on the streets of the city. Even here, in this place that thrives on sin and greed, the whiteness offers a certain sense of innocence. My family moves through the crowds of midtown. Snow collects in my mother's brown hair and on her black beret. She turns to me and smiles. Today, she is calm. My father walks with my sister, their hands interlocked. He slows his pace and takes hold of my hand, too. The three of us walk that way while my mother walks behind to watch over her family. My father and my sister laugh together and talk about how amazing Valerie is doing, now that she has been out of rehab for less than a week. My father squeezes my hand.

"Isn't she doing great, Ang?" he says.

I nod my head and pause long enough to kiss his cheek. If only we could see into the future. Less than a week from now, Valerie will experience her first of many relapses. On New Year's Eve, I will be away at a ski resort with friends. My parents will plan a humble, substance-free evening for them and Valerie.

But just before my mother will have the opportunity to serve Valerie a plate of crab legs, she will snap. She will run from the house, take her car and end up in a bar. My cell phone will ring around 1 a.m. Nutley Police Department. An accident. She's fine. Jars of pills. A lot of booze. She'll reenter rehab and begin again. Only, the next time she snaps, she will run farther—all the way from our town in New Jersey to Miami, where she has no home, no job, no friends. For the next year, she will live there, sleeping on stranger's pull-out beds. Back in New Jersey, my mother will lie awake in her bed nearly every night, her phone clutched tightly to her chest. My father will refuse to speak my sister's name.

"You really are doing great, Val. We're all so proud of you," my father says with pride. He turns to me and then briefly back to my mother.

"I'm proud of all of us. This family can survive anything," he says. "Love can help you to survive anything."

***

On a brisk Saturday morning during my senior year of high school, my father is arrested at our home. As most Saturday mornings, I woke, showered, gossiped on the phone with friends, and then slipped into my color guard uniform in preparation for a high school football game. I was in my bedroom when I heard the knock on the front door, followed by my mother's wails. Two officers entered our foyer. My mother threw her body to the ground and looked at my father in a way that suggested she was happy with his blatant crucifixion. I sat at the top of our stairwell and watched as one of the officers held my father's arms behind his back and then slipped metal handcuffs onto each of his wrists. My father briefly looked in my direction before the officers took him away.

He never let our eyes meet.

It was the first time in my life that I witnessed my father hang down his head in shame.

As a high school freshman and sophomore, my father attended all of my high school color guard performances, sometimes traveling hours across our state and across the country with my mother just to watch me shimmy in my sequins. He learned to notice the subtleties of my dance routines, so that he would have an encouraging comment to share with me after every performance.

"You looked great out there today," he would say through a grin. "You're pivots are becoming much stronger."

At every game he wore a button with a picture of me in my uniform pinned to his chest.

Following my mother's announcement about us traveling to my aunt's home up north, I pack only enough of my things to last me a weekend.

I stare out the car window as my mother speeds up the New Jersey Turnpike to the place where my new life will begin. The roads are dirty with slush; all the cars that rush past are covered in a layer of whitish filth.

When we arrive to my aunt's home—a multi-million dollar mansion in one of the most exclusive towns in the state—I find that my aunt has rearranged some things in her guest room, cleared out the dresser drawers, and filled the guest closet with enough clean towels and linens to last any guest several seasons. I expected a sheet thrown on the living room sofa, as she had always done during every visit of my life. This change is my first realization of the permanency of the situation.

I settle onto the bed—a fancy tuft of designer fabrics, rich with gold brocades. I've always known my aunt to be wealthy and it has never bothered me in the least. But now, seeing myself—my torn Converse sneakers, my faded Sex Pistols t-shirt—in this setting for more than a few days, makes me feel ill.

I reach for the phone to call my father. But I'm not sure where to reach him. At the place that, just hours ago, was our home? Then I remember that the last time I saw my father was on Christmas Eve. I had finished my shift at my part-time job and then waited on the curb for my father to pick me up. My manager, Henry, a homosexual in his early thirties who frequently comments on my hair and my makeup in ways that suggest he is prettier than me, waited beside me on the curb. He tapped his foot and looked down at his watch repeatedly.

"You can just go, Henry. I know he'll be here soon," I said, even though I didn't know for sure.

"I mean, it's Christmas Eve." It was all Henry could muster before he sprinted to his car, rubbing his hands together from the cold.

For more than an hour, I waited, alone, with no money, no access to a phone, and no jacket, in a dark, abandoned parking lot on Christmas Eve.

Eventually, my father's car rolled up and onto the curb, just inches from where I sat. I climbed in.

After a silent car ride, he parked on the street in front of our house. The windows were illuminated yellow squares. All up and down our street, holiday lights twinkled. The ground was dusted with a thin veil of snow.

I opened my car door.

"Aren't you coming?" I asked.

But my father remained silent.

"How can you not come inside? It's Christmas Eve?" I said again and let the tears fall. "Daddy, please. Mommy made dinner. Everyone is here. You have to cook us breakfast in the morning like you always do. It's our tradition. Daddy, please." I begged and looked desperately into the eyes of the man who I once equated with our Savior. The same eyes that mine are near replicas of.

"Tell your mother I'm sorry," he said.

"You're a sinner." It was all I could muster.

I exited the car and watched my father pull away down our street.

I click down the phone before it begins to ring. My mother calls for me from downstairs. When I find her, she has a cigarette pressed to her lips, even though she hasn't smoked since she was a teen.

"You should call one of your girlfriends and ask them to bring you up more of your things," she says and eyes my small overnight bag that I have left on the marble floor. "We're going to be here for a while."

***

My father is right, I think. *Love can help you to survive anything—except for this.*

My heart breaks when I look at my sister and notice the visible layer of oil and filth that hides her once enviable hair. To strangers, I'm certain this beauty *faux pas* goes unnoticed. But to me, it might as well be painted on one of the billboards in Times Square. It speaks volumes about the woman she has become.

My mind wanders backwards to a memory: It is the late 1980's. My sister is about seventeen and I am around nine years old. It is Christmas time and we are in New York, visiting from our home in New Jersey—an annual holiday tradition. My mother, my father, my sister and I wander through FAO Schwartz. I consume myself with a giant teddy bear that I pray my parents will let me keep. My sister, too old for toys, stands with my father. They lean together against a wall and watch me play. My sister has on a pair of tight, stonewashed designer jeans and a trendy black motorcycle jacket. Her thick, black Mediterranean hair falls heavily around her face and shines under the fluorescent lights of the store. Her eyes are concealed behind a pair of chic black sunglasses, which she never thought to lift onto her head when she entered the store. Her beauty is the sort that makes you stop to take a second look. I wrap the bear's arms around my body and make one of his paws wave in the direction of my family. As I do, I see a woman approach my sister. The woman motions with her hand for a pen. I watch Valerie lift her sunglasses and laugh, politely. Later, I learn this woman believed my sister, despite her short stature, was Cindy Crawford, and thus asked her for an autograph. After the woman walks away, embarrassed, my father locates a new toy—a sort of electronic Etch-a-Sketch.

He and my sister laugh together as my sister signs "Cindy Crawford" across the board in bold, cursive letters. I drop the bear's arms and run to my family. I grip my sister's hand as our family exits the store.

But today, the truth is that I'm ashamed to hold my sister's hand. She looks like the type of woman that, just a few years ago, we might have mocked together. The type of woman we would have passed on the street and called a train wreck or a disgrace. Today, my sister looks exactly like what she is: an alcoholic.

I try to focus on my mother's smile.

My family stops walking and pauses in front of the tree. We briefly reminisce about the farm the tree came from this year, a small place located in the heart of our hometown.

"Do you girls remember when your mother and I used to take you to that farm for *our* family tree every year?" my father says.

I think about it for a moment, caught in a daydream of me, at age five or six, running through the rows of evergreens, the branches tall above my body, and my teenage sister, playfully chasing after me with fistfuls of snow.

"It's pretty amazing to think they brought that tree all this way," my father says.

But what I want to say, what I believe each of us wants to say is *it's amazing to think that we have come all this way.*

To think that we have ended up here.

My father suggests we take a photograph. The four of us move into a line in front of the tree—the pride of our hometown, and, momentarily, the pride of our small family. A stranger snaps the picture for us—a still image of my mother, my father, my sister and me—at peace with one another in this singular moment. My mother squeezes my hand tighter than she has in months, kisses my face, and gently tucks my hair behind my ear, where it will keep safe from the winter breeze. She glances at each of us—this portrait of our family—satisfied. Her eyes water.

"This is all I ever wanted," she says and wraps her arms around Valerie and me. "This is everything I've ever wanted in this world."

The crowd begins to shove, anxious to stand in front of the tree themselves. Arms push, shoulders hit the bodies of strangers and, in a flash, the moment is gone. My family begins to walk towards Sixth Avenue. I glance back only once. Another family poses in the spot where, just seconds before, my family lived together in harmony. I turn back toward my family. I raise my right hand to my forehead, move it down to my chest and touch it to each of my shoulders to make the sign of the cross.

Pray for us, I whisper into the wind.

I wonder if the moment will mean as much to this new family as it did to my own.

A Pair to Draw To

By Terri Elders

Back in spring, 1955, when Mama invited me to join her and her lifelong best friend, Edith, at the kitchen table for a cup of coffee, I finally felt grown up.

"We need to plan the shower games," Mama said. If the two huddled over coffee, it usually signaled the onset of a woman-to-woman confab, no children allowed. But when my fiancé and I set our wedding date for mid-June, Edith stepped up to host my bridal shower. Donna, her daughter, who'd be my bridesmaid, had declined the role, citing shyness. I poured coffee for myself and took a chair.

"I've ordered a sheet cake from Helms," Edith said, alluding to the bakery truck that roamed our suburban streets each weekday afternoon.

Mama nodded. "I'll make deviled eggs and finger sandwiches. Ham salad and some watercress, since Lee thinks those are the bee's knees."

Mama and Edith exchanged slight knowing smiles, but

my jaw dropped. I nearly dropped the sugar spoon, as well.

"Auntie Lee? She's coming?"

"Yes." Mama's voice took on the same soothing tone she once used to persuade me to down a dose of cod liver oil. "She'll give you something lovely, too."

"Oh, Mama," I wailed, "she'll bray at her own jokes, use that affected British slang, and win all the pen and paper games and gloat about it."

Auntie Lee often compared herself to the comedienne Eve Arden. Both were long legged, fast talking, wisecracking women, but that's where the resemblance ended. In the years of my youth, I adored Arden as the sardonic teacher on the radio and TV show, *Our Miss Brooks*. But I could barely tolerate five minutes of Lee.

Unlike pert Miss Brooks, forever pursuing clueless Mr. Boynton, my horse-faced Auntie Lee already had her mate, Uncle Bernie, a lout if there ever was one. As long as I could remember, the couple played pinochle every other Saturday with my parents. I used to flee to my room to avoid them.

Bernie, who smelled of stale beer, greeted me with a pat on the fanny until I overheard Daddy tell him I was getting too old for that. Lee would draw me into a bear hug, emitting a sour scent, as if she needed a bath.

Mama once explained that Bernie was a nephew of Grandma's brother, Great Uncle Loring. Mama thought he was a second cousin, once removed. So far as I was concerned, he and Lee weren't removed nearly far enough. Even with my door shut, I could hear her triumphant screech whenever she took a trick at the Saturday card games.

Mama and Daddy admired Bernie because he somehow made a fortune at post WWII construction. Bernie and Lee spent lavishly, too. Their son, Billy, attended a costly private military academy, and when my folks dragged me over to their house a few months earlier, I had stared hypnotized at *Ford Theater* on their Westinghouse television, the first color broadcast I'd ever seen.

For their twenty-fifth anniversary, they flew to London so Lee could hobnob with distant relatives of her dainty mother, always referred to as The Duchess. That's when Lee started saying "cheerio" instead of "goodbye," and serving scones at supper instead of plain old baking powder biscuits.

"Well, what about games?" Edith asked, breaking the silence.

"How about famous pairs? That's always a hit. We supply the first name, and our guests have to write down the partner." Mama started scribbling on her notepad. "Let's see. There's Lum and Abner, Martin and Lewis, Abbot and Costello."

"We need to get some lovers in there, too," I said.

"Romeo and Juliet, Scarlett O'Hara and Rhett Butler, Bogie and Bacall." Mama paused.

Edith grinned, "Don't forget John Alden and Priscilla. We have to have one or two tough ones. And how about odds and ends?"

"Smith and Wesson?" I began, "The cat and the fiddle? Nip and tuck?"

"And one for Auntie Lee! The jack of diamonds and the queen of spades," Mama blurted out.

"What? Why one for her... and why are those cards a

pair?"

"That's a pinochle, the pair the game's named for," Mama said, "and it's always worthwhile to make Lee feel special. Nobody else is likely to know the answer, and you'll be glad on your wedding day if Lee has a good time at the shower."

I stared. This seemed so unlike Mama, so conniving, so manipulative, so... mercenary.

"Trust me, child," Mama said. "Nobody else can afford that set of stainless copper bottom pots and pans you've been hankering for, and I've already dropped a hint to Lee that you would love one."

The night of the shower Auntie Lee smelled as funky as ever, plus she wore a sleeveless blouse which gave us all a glimpse of her unshaven armpits. As I expected, she crowed as she won the first two games, piling up her bath salts and stationery prizes at the foot of her chair. I hoped she'd put the salts to good use. My college friends cast me sympathetic glances and chuckled at Lee's jokes, as I'd begged them in advance to do.

"Now for the final game and a special prize, we have famous pairs," Edith announced.

All heads bent over the game sheets. I noticed Auntie Lee finishing before the others, then glancing about the room. She went back and erased something, then settled back in her chair.

Edith read the results, and then asked who had more than ten correct answers. Five women raised their hands, including Lee. Twelve? Only three hands remained. Thirteen? Down to

Lee and shy Donna. Fourteen? The same two hands remained aloft. Fifteen? Lee lowered hers.

Mama handed a small package to Donna who simply beamed as she unwrapped a bottle of *Emeraude* cologne. "I've never won anything before," she announced. "I wouldn't have guessed the queen of spades if Mom hadn't taught me how to play pinochle last week."

Lee glanced at Mama. "Silly me forgetting those two were partners! I must be getting old."

I knew there was no way Lee didn't know that final answer, and so did Mama. Lee had chosen to let Donna win.

"Time for refreshments and presents," Edith trilled, heading for the kitchen.

I saved Lee's shower gift for last. I folded the luxurious white paper embossed with silver wedding bells, and set it aside. "Just perfect to line my lingerie drawer," I said.

Mama was right. Lee had selected sheer nylon pink baby doll pajamas, perfect for my honeymoon. This time I engulfed Lee in a bear hug. "Thanks so much," I whispered.

After the guests had left, I cornered Edith and Mama in the kitchen.

"Why did Auntie Lee let Donna win that prize? You know she knew the answer."

"Your Auntie Lee has a generous spirit and lots to put up with," Mama began. Edith nodded assent. "Billy goes to private school because he's so mean he's been expelled from three high schools. Bernie spends his days swilling beer and picking up bar flies. Lee's mother, that tiny Duchess, makes Lee feel like an awkward giraffe."

I must have looked astonished.

"Oh, grow up," Mama said.

 I think that's when I really did.

Stirrups

By Leslie Tucker

The backseat Olympic Games in my boyfriend's Mustang convertible were over, and I was in labor, stuck at a light in a rough Detroit neighborhood, because my mother had insisted I go to a hospital where no one she knew would recognize me. The stoplight near Seven Mile and Myers was fresh red as the drunk stumbled to the curb and pounded the windshield of my Ford Fairlane with his meaty fists. He hawked a mucus gob onto the window and tugged at the passenger door handle. "Spara fella some change whitey-girlie? Gimme a dolla, jus' a dolla, nize piece like you, I know ya gotta dolla..."

Eyes darting sideways, I ran the light, tires crunching broken glass as the drunk stumbled, fell and flipped me the bird in my rear view mirror. I guessed that the hospital was several blocks away, but which direction? The freeway exit off the Lodge was closed. I couldn't approach the Emergency Entrance as I'd practiced.

I sped up, hoping a cop would chase me, but cops avoided

urban-scorched earth, burned-out buildings, ramshackle bars with doors yawning onto vomit stained sidewalks, and dark streetlights, their lamps lost to target practice. An eighteen-year-old suburban honor student like me was about as safe as a dime bag of heroin on the pavement.

I crushed the accelerator as the pain stabbed my groin and warm liquid gushed onto the floor of the car, soaking my panties, Indian print gauze skirt, and shoes. The contractions were ten minutes apart when I'd left home an hour before, and the vise tightened in my lower abdomen as I hunched forward to squelch the pain. Elbows bent in tight "V"s, I gripped the steering wheel, mind churning, eyes scanning pockmarked street signs. I wished I had called someone, anyone, and told them I was headed downtown to have my baby.

Earlier, I'd awakened alone in my student apartment with the first contractions. I'd studied a library book and believed that first babies took ages to be born, so I showered, braided my sodden hair, and pulled an elasticized skirt over my belly. Lugging my turquoise Samsonite down stairs to the parking lot, I sat on it, doubled over as a contraction came and went. I'd call my parents from the hospital.

The Emergency Entrance sign came up fast on the wrong side of the road and I swerved across two lanes, squealed into the drive, and screeched to a halt at Grace Northwest. A Rent-a-Cop sucked his cigarette and ignored me as I left the car running and lumbered inside.

Dripping on the linoleum, rubber soles squeaking, I shifted my weight from foot to foot. I clutched my suitcase and scanned the jammed-up waiting room. Everyone was staring at me. One young woman paced, holding a bloody towel to her swelling face. Behind the desk, the behemoth receptionist glared.

"Is that your car blocking the door, Missy?"

"Yes, but I…"

Raising a ham-sized forearm, she aimed her index finger and thumb at me, hand gun style. "Well, you'll have to move it before we can do anything." Paralyzed, I didn't speak.

"Did you hear me, girl? You can't leave your car…"

"I can't move it. I'm wet and cold, and I drove here by myself, my water broke in the car and I'm having my baby any minute…"

The swollen-faced woman dropped her bloody towel, stuck her feet into rubber flip-flops, strutted over and stood by my side. Jaw jutting forward at the crank behind the desk, she waggled her finger, "Sista, you betta do somethin' for this girl, an' I mean now. You can damn well get that lazy-ass jamoke by the door to park her car for Chrise sake."

The old bat recoiled. My defender planted both hands on ample hips, "I said *now*, Sista, and I mean *now!*" The receptionist grabbed a filthy white phone, dialed two numbers, and a muscular orderly bounced up with a wheelchair.

"Siddown, honey. Ri-cheer. I'll get you upstairs. You jus' c'mon, siddown now."

I dropped into the chair.

"You hold your suitcase, girl. It's small." He plopped it down on my thighs. "Use both hands, girl. C'mon, hold on to it."

Rolling toward the elevator, the orderly hollered at a sullen janitor, another orderly, and a candy machine repairman. "Hey Bro! Whassup?" and, "How 'bout you, man, whassup wich you?" and, "Hey my man! Now you get that fixed. It be break time soon and I be needin' some suga." He pushed the elevator button and slurped a bottle of Coke. I lost the awkward grip on my suitcase and it clunked onto the floor.

"Aw c'mon girl, can't you hold that thing?"

He tossed his Coke into the trashcan, grabbed my suitcase, and we rode up six floors in silence. At the crowded nurse's station, his hundred-watt grin flashed as he bellowed, "Hey, Lucille! My, my, you lookin' fine today." She glowered. "Now, c'mon Lucille. You be nice to yo' man Leroy. Where you want this girl?"

"Ssshh…" she hissed. "Pipe down, Leroy. This is a hospital. Put her in 613 for now. We'll move her later."

Leroy pointed at the hospital gown on the bed. "You put that on now. Nurse be here sooner n' you want." Standing my suitcase on the floor, he spun his heels, slapped his palms on the wheelchair and pranced away.

One bare bulb dangled from the ceiling, a torn shade covered half the grimy window, and when I yanked the hospital gown around me, one of the ties tore off. I collapsed on the tightly made bed, too exhausted to turn down the covers, and tried to time my contractions. I didn't have a watch, and the clock on the wall never moved off 2:35.

What would happen now? I had imagined women learned from women, mothers exhaling answers into inquisitive daughters, sharing rituals, but it had been all secrets, all my life, between Mother and me. Proper, plant-leaf-dusting-lady vs. brainy-rebel-girl: no codes cracked.

I was breathing hard, holding off hysteria, when a candy striper came in and chirped, "You poor thing, this says you're here all by yourself. Can I call someone?"

I huffed out my parents' phone number.

In 1966, we women who went to hospitals for childbirth labored alone. Nurses and doctors dropped in, spread us open with cold steel speculums and measured our progress. Family members hovered nearby in waiting rooms, like in old Hollywood comedies—expectant fathers smoking, cracking jokes, waiting for congratulations from doctors. "It's a boy! And the little woman is just fine!" My parents arrived, were relegated to this limbo, and not allowed in my room, where I moaned, screamed, and "panted like a dog," the way the library book had instructed. Nimble-fingered nurses probed the dilation of my cervix, offered reassurance, "First babies take a long time to be born. You try and calm down, honey." I tried to be brave and stifled my sobs. The library book hadn't said exactly how long, a 'long time' was.

Weeks before, at dinner, Mother aimed her vocabulary across the Chippendale. "The pain will teach you a lesson, assuage your guilt." *Assuage*, Mother, really?

As a double medalist in wild behavior and naiveté, I was discovering in that hospital that life was more complex than backseats, book learning, and first impressions. From the handsome backseat boy to the bleeding black woman who rescued me in the ER, I got it. From my family's manicured, Birmingham neighborhood, to the terrifying, urban ghetto around the Detroit hospital, the emotional carnival roared on. With ferocious clarity, I realized that superficial judgments were rarely accurate.

Twenty hours later, my balding doctor swabbed his dripping forehead. "This is taking way too long, little mother, but then first babies generally do. I'm heading home. Meet Dr. Rajiv. He'll take good care of you."

Another three hours dragged by; finally, a sweat-drenched nurse cajoled me through three delirious pushes, and my baby's head slid out; one more and her shoulders broke free. Quivering, I heaved up onto my elbows and yanked the sheet off to get a glimpse. Bloody, and wrinkled like stale fruit, her exquisite features stunned me. The nurse growled, "We need to keep this area sterile; you lay down right now!" Then, in a gentle voice, "She's beautiful. Look at that rosebud mouth."

Someone lifted her from between my legs, laid her on a white metal table. They blotted her off, inserted a rubber bulb in her tiny nose and pumped. She screamed, my spine tingled, and I vowed to splash sweetness all over this girl of mine, breathe love into her every day, inflate her with courage and confidence. Tears soaked my hairline, ran into my ears, and someone tossed a blanket over me. My eyes clamped shut, blocked out the blinding overhead lights, and I dissolved into sleep, my feet still in the stirrups on the stainless steel table.

The Meaning of Abortion

By Jennifer Levy

Everything is relative to a thirteen-year-old girl. This is a time in a girl's life when environmental factors play a defining role in your state of happiness. For me, this was an extremely difficult time.

I grew up with my mother, grandmother and grandfather in a two bedroom apartment in an affluent neighborhood. Unlike any of my friends, I shared a small bedroom with my mother and slept on a trundle bed at her feet. Although my relationship with her was more like that of two sisters than a mother and daughter, like all teenage girls coming into their own, I yearned for privacy. I was incredibly envious of my friends' seemingly perfect lives.

This jealousy was largely a result of a constant self-imposed comparison. I just couldn't help but notice what my friends had that I did not. My mother drove a pea soup, or vomit color as I referred to it then, 1970-something Ford Pinto. My friends' parents drove new Mercedes, BMWs, or other foreign-made, shiny cars with beautiful leather interiors, every bell and whistle and that unmistakable "new car smell." I lived in a small, cramped apartment that was owned by my grandparents and was decorated with the trappings of a Jewish matriarch that had kept everything handed down to her for generations. The carpet was old, grey and dingy with wrinkles running the entire length of the apartment from wear and tear. There was horrible pastel wallpaper in the kitchen and depressing grey flower prints in both bathrooms. In each room, the wallpaper peeled a little more every year and was brilliantly illuminated by harsh fluorescent lights, which showed every imperfection. Closet space was nonexistent and of course there was no room for a bike, large toys or sports gear. And having an animal, forget about it. My friends on the other hand lived in large single-family homes with huge immaculate kitchens and family rooms able to accommodate a sleepover party for twenty. There was always a private area for us kids to play independent of parents. They had all the latest and greatest toys and electronics, and some even had computers. Some girls had their own private bathroom attached to their bedroom, but all of them were able to decorate their bedrooms as they pleased. Their bedrooms were truly their own private oasis and they spent the majority of their time there. My friends participated in every camp, ski trip and extracurricular activity offered and had the very best equipment that money could buy. At thirteen years old the list of things that my friends had that I did not was endless.

One summer day, angry with the world that I wasn't able to participate in a camping trip with my friends because we did not have the money, I got into a fight with my mother. At first, I pleaded my case and explained that I simply had to go, *everyone would be there*. Then, I offered to sell my favorite piece of jewelry that I had received as a birthday present, to finance the trip. When my mother still refused to give into my argument, I yelled and screamed complaining about how unfair my life was and that it was all her fault. Finally, I looked her dead in the eye with my face twisted in anger and said, "I hate you."

My mother was always patient with me and rarely lost her cool, but these words pushed her over the edge. She grabbed me by the arm and scolded me for acting like a spoiled brat. Then, in an eerily calm voice she said, "Honey, I am doing my very best. I want you to have all the things your heart desires, but that's not always possible." Finally, in an irritated voice, she said that she would try to make the camping trip happen, but said that she couldn't make any promises. When my mother made a promise, she always kept it. On the other hand, when she told me that she "couldn't make any promises," I knew that I was not going to get what I wanted. I was mad, the kind of mad that you can't control. With both middle fingers pointed straight in the air, I told my mother she was a bitch. Without raising an eyebrow, or even her voice, she explained that my behavior was unacceptable and my phone was being taken away. The phone to a thirteen-year-old girl is like water to a camel, it is lifeblood. It is the essence that keeps you going, especially in times of turmoil. I stormed out of the house, saying nothing.

This was the first time I had ever run away and was not

sure where to go. I tried the few friends I had in the adjoining neighborhood, but the apartment complex I lived in might as well have been a senior living facility. No one was home and after a few hours of walking around insulated, boring, suburbia, looking at the same condos and townhomes and the same landscaping on every block, I was hot and tired and had cried myself a river. I wanted nothing more than to go home. But, my pride wouldn't allow it. I crossed the street into the adjoining neighborhood of townhouses. They seemed so big, sitting in their freshly painted white gazebos, surrounded by purple and pink pansies, I thought about how unfair my life was. Beauty surrounded me. It was within my reach, but I couldn't touch it. I came to the conclusion that I was doomed to be unhappy and the root of that unhappiness was the place I lived. Finally, hours after I stormed out my front door, I returned home. With only one foot in the door, my infuriated grandparents began scolding me. My mother, who rarely stood up to her parents, who had taken us in when I was only one year old, grabbed my hand and dragged me into the kitchen, sternly telling them to back off. "She's my daughter. I'll handle it."

She shut the door leading into the living room and asked me to sit down. When she turned around there were tears in her eyes, which she quickly wiped away. She breathed a sigh of relief and quietly spoke. "Jennifer, you are my world. There is nothing I wouldn't do for you and nothing we can't work out together. Please don't ever leave again. If something had happened to you, I just don't know." Again, her eyes welled up and she hugged me like we had been apart for years, instead of hours. When she finally released me from her embrace, she told me she loved me and asked what would make me happier. I don't think she was prepared for my response: "I want to live with dad."

The relief I saw on her face just minutes before immediately disappeared. With fear in her eyes, and sadness in her voice, she simply asked, "Why?"

I explained that I believed wholeheartedly that my unhappiness was a result of where we lived. I was jealous of everything and everyone around me and there was no escape. As always, my mother listened intently as I spoke. Occasionally, she would reach out and gently caress my hand, assuring me things would work out, without ever speaking a word. She told me that I didn't know my father like she did and she thought it was a bad idea. Regardless, if that was what I really wanted, she would make the call. The choice was mine. "Please call him," I said.

My father and I did not have your typical father-daughter relationship. We saw each other only once or twice a year and spoke on the phone infrequently. When my mother handed me the phone, my stomach began to churn. After a couple minutes of chit chat, I found the courage to ask him if I could come live with him.

After a long pause, he cleared his throat and said, "I could never take you away from your mother. Why don't you come and see me and, if you want, spend the rest of the summer here with me." *It was start. Maybe I could convince him to make it permanent once I was there and he saw how great I was.* Regardless, I was thrilled and couldn't pack my bags fast enough. A week later, I kissed and hugged my mother goodbye as I prepared to board the plane to Chicago. She looked at me holding back her tears and said, "Just remember, I'm only a phone call away."

With the excitement of new surroundings and a possible new life in front of me, I replied, "Stop worrying about me. I'll be fine."

My father lived in a suburb of Illinois, about forty-five minutes outside of Chicago. He owned a catalog business that provided sub-standard, crappie toys, probably made by children in China working sixty hours a week for pennies, as prizes for kids in the Boys Scouts, school book-a-thons and sports leagues. He was married to his second wife, who was a bit of a blond bimbo and wanted me to call her "Mom two." He had two dogs, an Old English Sheep dog and a Toy Poodle, lived in a single family home, had nice cars and lived a fairly comfortable lifestyle.

Upon my arrival at O'Hare Airport, my father and I went into the city. Despite this being my third time in the city, it had not lost its allure. Chicago was like nothing I had ever experienced before. I loved it. The skyscrapers went on forever and seemed to disappear in the clouds. The hustle and bustle of the cars, cabs and the L were a sensory overload in the most wonderful way, even the exhaust and the pollution they produced was exhilarating. We walked through the heart of the city before landing at a 50's style restaurant, where we decided to have lunch. As I walked down the city streets, I felt at home amongst the chaos of the city. I remember thinking how great it was to feel unknown, to make random decisions, to be unnoticed.

After lunch, my father and I got into his new car. He was always a bit of car fanatic and had just purchased a Grand National, which he explained to me was a car driven by FBI agents, specifically for high-speed chases. A seemingly uninteresting car, it was black and non-descript. It looked much like a Buick sedan, but it went zero to sixty in five seconds, which I got to experience on the way home. As if that wasn't frightening enough, when we got back to his house, "Mom two" was waiting with outfits she had bought for me. After begrudgingly trying on some of the ugliest clothing I have seen to date, we all had dinner together.

While "Mom two" did dishes, I got ready for bed and popped a movie in the VCR. I slept on a sleep couch in the living room at my father's house because the other three bedrooms were filled with junk. Halfway through the movie, my father came downstairs alone and turned off the TV. Sitting on the edge of the sleep couch, he asked what was going on at home between my mother and me. When I began to complain about her, he stopped me in an abrupt fashion and in an authoritative tone said, "I want you to listen to me very carefully." Then, in a calm softer voice he continued, "If it wasn't for your mother, you wouldn't be here today."

I didn't get it. "What does that mean, dad?" His response would shape the rest of my days.

"Do you know what an abortion is?" he asked me. When I said I did not, he explained it to me in detail, an explanation I could have done without. But if that wasn't bad enough, he then told me the reason for his question.

My mother and father were never married. When my mother found out that she was pregnant with me, my father presented her with two options. One, she could abort the fetus, marry him, prince charming, and live happily ever after. Two, she could have the baby without him. He did not want children. The conversation pretty much ended there as I found myself speechless for the first time in my young life. My father told me to think about things and have a good night.

Feeling unloved and unwanted in an unfamiliar environment, I couldn't even think about sleeping. Once I was certain my father and his wife were asleep, I picked up the phone and called my mother. It was late and her voice was tired when she picked up the phone. When she heard my voice, she asked if everything was ok. I told her I was fine, but wanted to come home as soon as possible. She told me that she would get me on a flight the following day and asked if I wanted to talk. I told her that I just wanted to come home. She told me she'd see me tomorrow and said goodnight. I hung up the phone feeling relieved. The next day, I was on a plane heading home as promised.

On the plane ride, I thought about the sacrifices my mother had made for me. She had given up her chance at love. Despite an illness, which was making every day activities hard for her, she always found the energy to keep me involved in my numerous hobbies, like gymnastics, baton and softball. She never complained and gave up any luxuries for herself in order to give me the little extras, like a Cabbage Patch Kid doll that I simply *had* to have. By the time I arrived home, I was riddled with guilt. Exiting the plane, I saw her waiting for me and ran into her arms. With tears in my eyes, I told her I loved her and I was sorry.

"What for?" she asked.

"I didn't know," I responded as I held her tightly.

"Know what?" she asked.

"How good I have it. I love you."

Sex Education

By Jennifer Tress

When my mom was pregnant with my younger sister, I asked her where babies came from. She told me matter-of-factly that when a man's penis becomes aroused he enters it into a woman's vagina. Once there, sperm is released. It travels to the woman's womb where an egg is deposited, and—if all goes well—fertilizes and becomes a baby. "Well," she qualified, conspiratorially, "I guess when a man is aroused he doesn't *always* enter a woman's vagina, but let's save that story, shall we?" I looked at her curiously. I was four.

To further explain, she pulled out a copy of *Our Bodies, Ourselves*, the women's health bible of that time, and showed me diagrams of reproductive organs and procedures. Filled with a new world of information, I turned to pen and paper to process. The "Sex Papers," still in my possession, contain many insights into the mind of a small child obsessed with sex. One depicts two naked people sitting across from each other smiling and smoking cigarettes. Another is of a cheerleader cheering.

Every paper has the word "sex" at the top of the page.

I quickly moved from my drawing phase to play-acting and casting my toys and Star Wars action figures in an ongoing production called "Mash Your Privates." This involved me holding two figures, one in each hand, making them face each other and clacking their plastic torsos together in a savant-like fashion.

These are the pairings that made sense to me:

Leia and Luke,

Storm Trooper and Storm Trooper,

Obi Wan and Yoda,

C3PO and R2D2,

Han Solo and Chewbacca, and

Weeble Wobble and Barbie.

For the most part, my parents allowed me to explore this curiosity unhindered. That is until one day when I was mashing the privates of my Donnie and Marie Osmond dolls. My mom walked past this scene with a basket full of laundry, and yelled, "For God's sake, Jenny, they're brother and sister!" She muttered incomprehensively as she carried the basket upstairs. I paused for a minute and looked at their frozen, innocent, smiling faces and their matching pink, purple and tan outfits and reasoned: *Well, so are Luke and Leia*, and went back to the mashing.

Of course, none of this had any connection whatsoever with the euphoria that comes with feeling turned on. I didn't know what that was until I saw my first Prince video: "Little Red Corvette." I watched, rapt, as he batted his Bambi-like eyes and subtly gyrated with the microphone stand, looking right into the camera and my soul. I didn't quite *get* what this feeling was, but I definitely thought a lot about that tiny, androgynous sexpot at night while I wrestled with the sheets.

These wrestling matches started on a random night when I was around thirteen and was tossing and turning when the sheet glided between my legs and I froze. *What the hell was that?* I proceeded to perform the move 58 more times to see if I could get to the bottom of the mystery. I didn't at first, but it was fun trying.

When *Purple Rain* was released, I went with two friends to the movie theater. We told our parents we were going to see *Gremlins* and bought tickets to that show, but snuck into the back of the already darkened theater showing *Purple Rain*. We were not prepared. We gripped our armrests tightly, mouths hanging open as we watched Prince finger fuck Apollonia and the stars interpret various songs like "Sex Shooter," and "Darling Nikki," where Prince vigorously dry humps his microphone stand on stage. It was way too much for our porous minds. What was I thinking, jumping from dolls bumping plastic uglies straight to Prince and the Revolution in one move? I went home after that movie completely confused and freaked out, yet also excited to "hit the sheets."

"Jenny, are you OK?" My mom asked when I got home. "You don't look so good."

"No, I'm fine, just tired. I'm going to go to bed."

"How was *Gremlins?*"

I looked directly at her. "Some parts were really, really weird."

That night, amidst the sheets, I thought about the scene with Prince and Apollonia. Instead of stopping when I reached the point of near unbearable pleasure—it felt like being tickled—I kept going. *Did I pee?* I felt the sheets, but nothing was overly wet. For a while, I kept it my own little secret and took lots of "naps."

My friends and I didn't talk about stuff like this when we were thirteen. I think we realized we knew next to nothing about it. We were in that odd, short phase between leaving childhood behind and committing to being teens. We were scared to admit to, or share, anything that made us look like the weird kid—unless we knew we weren't alone. I always had respect for the kids who were the first to admit they were cutters, or who had bad home lives; you could almost physically see a wave of relief wash over the people who were present for a confession. Now they had an opening to say: "I had no idea. Me too."

This was also the stage in life when most of us had to attend health class, that awful period of sitting through uncomfortable lectures, and, in my class, overhead projector diagrams. My junior high health teacher tried to make these lectures fun by doing things like drawing his own overhead slides to guide a particular topic. One that stands out as the most embarrassing was the slide he used to explain the ovulation process. He drew an airplane with an egg jumping out of it yelling "Ovulaaatttioooon!" as it pulled its parachute. He did this slowly while he stood at the front of the class in his white polo shirt and tight, navy blue polyester shorts. He raised his hand up to simulate the slow, swaying back and forth of an object gliding safely to the ground. All he got for his trouble was the sound of silence. You could hear the crickets.

At fourteen my breasts grew from an A cup to a C cup seemingly overnight, which thrilled my younger sister. Whenever I was being bossy, she retorted by sticking her fists under her t-shirt, and stretching the material out to make them look like huge, lopsided breasts and saying "whatever" in the brattiest tone possible. At first I'd lunge, ready to throttle her, but that only seemed to egg her on so I soon turned the tables. "These puppies?" I'd say, pointing to my chest. "They're comin' for you, too."

This transformation made males of all ages take notice. This later brought on the epiphany that many men are rendered powerless in the presence of big boobs, but at fourteen it only made my stomach churn. I tried to hide them under numerous Firenza shaker knit sweaters from the Limited, which I color coordinated with my stirrup pants. Sometimes male teachers would call me and other well-endowed girls up to their desk and ask about our weekend while they stretched back in their chairs, arms behind their heads, spreading their legs apart.

Health class ended the same year we completed junior high and our teacher decided to close out the course with a talent show. It might have made more sense to put on a show with acts relevant to things we learned, like short plays inspired by Madonna's "Papa Don't Preach," but instead it was just a run of the mill talent show. Still in our Prince phase, my friend and I decided we should pair up and do an interpretive dance to "When Doves Cry." We practiced for hours in her screened-in porch, choreographing every last move and settling on outfits of royal blue satin shorts that went down to our mid-thighs, white tank tops, and overly permed hair with lace bows and lots of make-up. We looked like clown boxers.

As we clumsily performed the routine, accidentally elbowing each other, our health teacher went from watching us intently to cheering us on for our creativity and heart. I don't remember anyone winning but upon recently recalling this with a couple friends from high school, I could almost see one of the girls dusting off the cobwebs in her mind then shouting, "Oh my God, I *SAW* that show." She didn't sound pleased.

At sixteen I started working at a local video store. In the mid-eighties Blockbusters had sprung up in nearly all suburban areas, but small towns like Newbury did not warrant such an investment. Instead, I worked at a store called Stop N' Go Video, which was about 700 square feet and located in a strip mall. After I got the initial and brief training, I worked my shifts alone and was responsible for closing out the cash register and securing the store. Often, my friends would visit and we'd watch movies that were PG enough to withstand any potential customer's taste meter.

At least, that was, until I discovered a system for the porn. We didn't have enough space for a back room to store the X-rated box covers, so Stop N' Go's solution was to create a binder with either the video boxes flattened in the laminate sleeves, or promotional fliers from the distribution companies. Patrons would have to come to the front counter and ask for "the binder" to flip through and make their selection, which was located under the cash register.

This created countless embarrassing situations, where the customer was forced to peruse such titles as *Anal Annie and Magic Dildo* or *Whore of the Worlds* at the front desk while I diverted my attention to *anything* else, such as furiously cleaning the phone. Many times, parents of friends or even teachers would enter the store, see that it was me working, spend some time looking through the "family" genre row and then turn to me and say, "Looks like I've seen everything, Jen," before walking out. Yeah right, I thought. See you next time.

I also encountered several boys, some as young as thirteen, trying to rent the tapes. I'd humor them and ask for their IDs and they'd make up some lame excuse. But every once in a while, if I knew they were at least fifteen and terribly bookish, I'd let them flip through the binder first before asking for identification. In those rare instances, I felt justified that by giving them what I was sure was an infrequent glimpse at a naked woman; I was somehow better preparing them to deal with the fairer sex in the future.

My girlfriend Nicki and I, however, were the biggest viewers of the porn. Curious after giggling over the binder ourselves, we'd graduated to viewing movies in the store's VCR late at night. We learned about moves and positions in that video store by viewing the tapes and asking each other questions to clarify our understanding. "Ew! Are we supposed to *like* that when we get older?" I asked after viewing a particularly messy escapade. And even more personal questions, including, "Do you do that with Dan?"

"The Pearl Necklace? No! God, *Gross!*" she'd say as she rewound the scene for the 16th time.

I'd try out expressions and inflections I'd learned, purring porn phrases at odd times to my boyfriend from junior year to graduation. "Yeah, you like that don't you?" I'd ask as I kissed him. "You're a bad, bad boy."

He'd look at me strangely, saying something like, "Uh, yeah, I guess so." And we'd continue to make out, with me thinking all the while that the scenario would be even sexier if the pizza delivery guy showed up.

Viewing and studying women in porn became the template for what I assumed men perceived as desirable: arched backs, slightly parted mouths and closed-eyed moans. The fact that I'd been schooled in this area by Nina Hartley and Tracy Lords may have been undetectable by mere high school boys, but it gave me that extra swagger; something I knew would be uncorked with the right partner who respected all parts of me.

This was not to be the case my first time. When I was a sophomore, I had an unrequited crush on a senior who ran with the popular crowd, but had an outsider depth to him. He rarely talked to me, but some of his friends dated some of my friends so we'd see each other at parties on the weekends, where he drank a lot and went upstairs with numerous girls.

He was thickly built, tall and muscular and wore tight, dark tank tops under flannel shirts. He had dark, slightly curly hair, large hazel eyes, lush lips and face stubble that got heavier as the day wore on. He commanded drinking games and made people laugh. But he also looked melancholy and far away sometimes. He seemed to me a boy that needed saving; and he seemed to see something special in me, too. When I'd enter a room, he would look at me, without smiling, for ten whole seconds, and I would return the gaze until he broke it. He always broke it first. I thought we were communicating something in a secret code only we could understand and that all of it meant love and passion.

At one of these parties he asked me what I was doing after school on a Tuesday.

"Nothing."

"Want to hang out at my house?"

"Yeah, sure."

"Cool."

I told my Mom that I was volunteering to decorate the basketball team's lockers; instead, I met him in the parking lot after school and went to his place. We drank some of whatever his parents had the most of in their liquor cabinet—I think it was vodka, and watched TV for about an hour. Then he stood up, grabbed my hand and led me to his bedroom, which was small, sparsely decorated, and had two twin beds in it. He laid me down on one of them and immediately got on top of me and began to kiss me and press his crotch roughly down on mine—a real-life game of "Mash Your Privates!"

He grabbed my hands with his, raising them over my head. Then he reached down and grabbed my shirt, raising it over my head and tossing it on the floor. Then he took his shirt off and laid back down on me and continued to kiss me. A minute later he got off me and said in a quiet voice, while looking directly at me: "Take your pants off."

I did as commanded while he put on a condom and then laid fully on me and entered me. I was so "in the moment" that I couldn't even recall my porn training. I stared over his shoulder up at the ceiling, wincing a bit in pain and wondering when the "feel good" part was going to happen. *But still,* I thought, *it's with him.* In a few minutes, it was over. He got off me, looked down at a small dark red spot and asked whether I needed a towel. I looked down and saw that I did. He started to get dressed and so I followed suit and then he said, "I should probably take you home; my Mom'll be here soon."

"Ok, cool." He drove me back home, but dropped me off about a quarter of a mile from my house and said, "You can walk from here, right?"

"Of course I can," I said, my M.O. at that time being to have a stiff upper lip and project an air of not giving a shit, whether or not it was true. I just thought that was the way these interactions went.

"Thanks so much for the ride." I got out of the car, feeling at the time like I was different. *I'm a woman now,* I thought. I entered my house and drifted past my Mom who was cooking dinner and into my sister's room where she was playing with her toys. "Well hello, young lady," I said to her. "Did you finish your homework?"

"Shut up. Did you?"

"Ah, sweet, young Becky. There's so much of the world you haven't seen…" and then I lay down on the bed and stared into space. "So much to *learn.*"

The next day at school, he hardly even talked to me. The only acknowledgement was a head tilt as he passed me in the hall and a monotone "what's up?"

What's up?!? I just gifted you with my virginity is what's UP.

Doesn't that at least deserve a walk to my next class or a sharing of a cigarette out by the football field, asshole? That's what I wanted to say, but instead I returned the head tilt, said "not much" and ducked into the nearest bathroom to cry.

Looking back I believe those soulful stares were merely tacit recognition that for him, I was a sure thing. The only truly remarkable part about the experience was that he didn't care.

A few weeks after this, my Mom took me for my annual checkup with the doctor, who was also my pediatrician from way back. She explained that this appointment was going to be a little different than the others; that this one was going to be more of the gynecological nature.

I took all of this in and thought, *Ok, so the guy who's examined me since I was a baby is now going to be sticking his fingers in my vagina.* My next thought was, *Oh God! Oh God, he's going to know I'm not a virgin anymore! He's going to stick his hands in my vagina and immediately feel that my hymen is broken and then gasp and pull out his hand in shock and look at my Mom.*

"What?!?" she'll ask startled.

"Your daughter," I imagined him saying, "is no longer your sweet little angel." And my Mom will look at me and cry a single, disappointed tear, like that Native American in the 70's anti-litter ad campaign who saw you throwing your McDonalds's bag on I-480.

"Mom I'm not a virgin!" I screamed and my Mom slammed on the breaks amidst angry honks and pulled over on the side of the road.

"What? Who? When? Are you sure? Are you OK? Do you want to talk about it? Who?"

"Mom, it was a boy at school," I said crying. "He doesn't like me. It was only once. And I will NEVER, EVER do it again!" My mom hugged me and stroked my hair. "He wouldn't have been able to tell," she said, referring to the doctor's appointment. Five months later, another boy and I were exclusive and sexually active.

Lucky for me, this boy built the bridge between being treated poorly by a partner and being treated kindly and gently. I'm grateful to him for that early imprint on my brain. But, the sex was still…high school sex. It wasn't until twenty seven or twenty eight that I had the "I'll have what she's having" moment and I'm so grateful for that as well, because once you have that experience, you can never go back. And thank God for that.

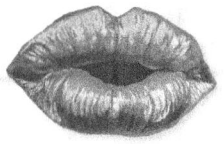

The Secret Suitcase

By Tammy Dietz

Fall of 1980
McKinley Junior High

Mr. Bittle thumbed his strawberry-blond mustache as he watched me walk toward him. His face was cast in shadows from the gray morning light filtering through the paneled windows behind him. When I reached his large metal desk, he set both hands palms down and smiled. I smiled back, and then slid behind the wooden flip-top desk directly facing him. The blue of his eyes sparked and he twitched.

His twitch: Every twenty seconds or so, his head tilted abruptly to one side, his lips jerked in a smirk, and one eye squeezed shut in a harsh blink. Nobody cared about his twitch, though. We all made more fun of Mrs. Hoffstedler—AKA Heatmizer—and her bright orange hair than we did Mr. Bittle and his twitch.

He was a very popular teacher and I was thrilled to be his

"favorite student." I'd met him the year before when I'd joined a Peer Counseling program that he sponsored. Along with other interested students, we'd spent two afternoons each week in Group discussing home life, teachers, and friends. Before the year was out, Mr. Bittle and I had struck up a friendship of sorts, meeting after school in his classroom on the days we didn't meet in Group. Over the summer, I'd thought about him often and that morning, the first day of eighth grade and well before the first-period bell would ring, I suppose I wasn't surprised to see the metal door of Room 41 propped open. But when I saw him behind his desk, as if waiting for me, my insides swirled.

Our eyes still intact, he lifted an envelope hidden beneath his hands. He set it at the edge of his desk, spun it around so the printing faced out, and nudged it toward me. "To Tammy," it said. It was so strange to see my name like that, on a letter from a man. One hand returned to his face where he stroked his mustache with his thumb and forefinger. His eyes stayed on me.

I opened the envelope and removed a card. A cartoon bear held flowers with a caption that read, "Next time, don't stay away so long. I've missed you." Inside, it said:

My Dear Tammy,
I am surprised by my feelings for you. I've thought of you all summer long. I'm so glad to see you again.
Love, Mr. Bittle

I smiled and put the card in my backpack, shrugged my

narrow shoulders and shifted in the desk. I loved him, too, I thought. Love was not a word used in our family, ever really, and for that reason, I didn't think much of it. I loved dancing. I loved church. I loved macaroni and cheese. And, I loved Mr. Bittle.

Yet, I thought about that card often that day. And whenever I had a moment alone, I took it out and ran the tips of my fingers over the printing as though I were reading Braille. No one had ever spoken to me that way. Nothing had ever made me feel so special. I was charged with an energy I didn't recognize, feeding every inch of my being from a center I didn't know I had right out to the new and fine hairs sprouting from odd places—arms, legs, armpits, and down there, too.

That night, I found an old vintage-looking suitcase in my father's junk room; it was tucked in a cupboard beneath an old black typewriter. I replaced the typewriter on the shelf and closed the cupboard door halfway, just as I found it, and then I brought it to my bedroom. Inside were three black and white photos of people I did not recognize and a Utah State University commencement brochure from 1959. I set these things aside to discard them in the backyard trash can, sure that no one would miss them, and then I placed the bear card inside, closed the lid, snapped the buttons shut, and slid it under my bed as far as it would go. I crouched and peeked at it with one eye and decided it was still vulnerable to discovery, so I took the rattiest towel from the hall closet and flung it under the bed and over the suitcase, until it looked like a pile of nothing but something to clean.

Winter of 1980
LDS Menlo Park Stake Center

Over the holidays a special meeting for young women only was held at the Mormon Stake House. Church members were organized by geography, the smallest unit being a Ward, with three or more Wards occasionally joining together to form a Stake and meet in a larger designated meeting house. The Young Women's conference included girls between twelve and eighteen from an even larger geographical area, hundreds of girls from as far as Monterey. Dresses and pantyhose, pumps, purses, delicate hands in laps, rows and rows of wooden pews filled with youthful beauty. And from the pulpit, as would have been the view by the female church leaders giving the talks that evening, a field of soft blow-dried hairstyles with bright bows and clips like wild flowers.

The conference began with a hymn and a prayer delivered by one of the few men present, a bishop from another Ward, and then the women took over. Three talks were given that day, on subjects related to setting and achieving clean, worthwhile goals using our *Behold Thy Handmaiden* workbooks. There was talk about recipes, learning new domestic crafts such as knitting or sewing, and volunteer work to help those in need.

And then a young Relief Society President from another Ward who looked like she might have been in her twenties gave the closing talk, which started out rather curious. She began by speaking about men and the importance of missionary work. But, she said, as important as it was for our priesthood holders to reach those in other countries and share the One True

Gospel with them, some young men would never make it on a mission. Men must be pure of heart and deed and this was not easy for men to do. This is where we young women came in. It was our "duty" and we would soon learn it would also be our "greatest challenge" to keep these young boys worthy.

"Girls, I want you to consider this rose."

She held up a single long-stemmed red rose, its shape unmistakable even from a distance.

"What a beauty to behold," she said into the microphone. "Now, what if I were to remove a petal from this rose? Just one petal won't make a difference, right?"

She removed a petal. And darn it if the rose didn't already look different.

"What if I remove another?" She removed another petal. "And another. And so on. And so forth." She plucked away at each petal, slow and deliberate, until she reached the last.

"Oh dear," she said, chuckling. "Look at what's left."

The remaining petal slumped against the stem in spite of her exaggerated attempts to raise it. She set the mutilated rose on the podium and folded her hands.

"Girls, *you* are this rose," she said. "This rose could be *you*."

She read a poem about love and grace and the Kingdom of Heaven.

"Just as the rose is perfect in the Lord's sight, so, too, are you. But when we allow ourselves to be spoiled and defaced, we sin in a manner that cannot be recovered. For once our flower is plucked, it is no more. It cannot regrow its petals. It does not regain its beauty. Its lovely scent is but a memory. It is useless."

The congregation sat silent, frozen. Perhaps some had already sinned and feared being singled out. Perhaps others were contemplating sin. And perhaps some were as confused by the message as I was. It's not that I didn't trust this woman with her Nancy Reagan hairdo and her baby blue ruffled collar. It's just that I couldn't imagine *being* her, having that much composure, confidence and grace. But most puzzling was that I couldn't find the logic in her words and so although I understood their gravity, I could not glean their meaning. Each time I tried to follow a logical lead, such as keeping the boys worthy, things would take a contradictory turn, such as how important we as women were and how we must find our own personal calling. How could both be true?

She finished her talk with mushy words about love of Christ and God and our living prophet and the One True Gospel and it went on, further clouding the message about that rose. My thoughts wandered to Mr. Bittle. By then, my secret suitcase was half full. He'd given me dozens more cards and personal letters as well. And books: *Jonathan Livingston Seagull* and a book of Shakespeare love sonnets that were as mind-numbing as sermons, but evocative, too. On some level I understood that our relationship must be our secret, but inside I felt ready to burst with the news that I'd secured such attention from a man. And I wondered what he would think of my church, if he would still consider me special when surrounded by all these other pretty young girls.

"And I'll conclude today with a gift for each of you."

Her amplified voice, sweet and high, echoed through the

large chapel. About a dozen girls stood in the congregation and moved out to the aisles. Each wore white and each carried a flat basket piled with white, long-stemmed roses.

"You are receiving these roses as my gift to you to show my faith in your dedication to purity and chastity and to the young men we must keep wholesome."

The girls in white divided and fanned out, giving handfuls of flowers to the girls seated at the ends of each row.

"Keep this rose to remember just how very special you are."

And there was the contradiction again. Every single rose seemed exactly the same.

The girls in white worked fast, but the pews were long, perhaps forty or more girls seated on long wooden benches. By the time I received my rose, its silky soft petals had already begun to show the tattered signs of age, and its small white head drooped like an apology.

Spring of 1981
123 Madison Avenue

It was the first openly rebellious thing I'd ever done. I'd stolen things, exchanged dirty secrets with trusted girlfriends, and once I'd plagiarized a poem for a class assignment. And of course there was Mr. Bittle. But all of those things could be hidden, disguised, or dismissed—explained away and kept to myself. Pierced ears, however, by their very design were meant to draw attention. Every girl I knew had pierced ears, even Mormon girls, and Dad could never explain why he didn't want me to have them as well. His mouth would turn down into an unmoving frown and his forehead would crinkle, as if the very request was shameful.

But I'd done it anyway, finally, after many pleas and just as many refusals and when news of my pierced ears reached Dad, there was a fight between my parents. I sat on my bed and listened while doors slammed, my father hollered, and my mother cried and apologized before turning bitter.

This was how it often went between them. Dad roared and threatened, even manhandled, and Mom cried like a child and begged to be left alone. The fight would come to end with cutting words from her, always from her. With each slice, he grew more silent and as he grew silent, the cuts went deeper.

He was a slob around the house.

"Now that's enough Sylvia. I've had just about enough. This is *my* house. I own this house."

Why couldn't he get a real job, like the rest of the men at church?

"Sylvia... I... I... I am an educated engineer..."

And what about his status at church? Any real man taking care of his family and home would have a Priesthood position of status and would be important to the Ward.

The front door closed shortly after that. He left. Her bedroom door closed and locked as well. And then the muttering began. This was also typical.

I touched the burning hot flesh of my ears with both hands and felt the tiny gold-plated studs, then fetched my suitcase from beneath my bed, pressed the rusty snaps and flipped the lid back flat. Just beneath the white rose from church, now dried to a keepsake, was the most recent card Mr. Bittle had given me. Dorothy and Scarecrow stood opposite one another in a colorful photo, Dorothy in tears and Scarecrow wearing a sideways smirk. The caption read, "I'm going to miss you most of all." And on the left, he'd written that it was he who would be missing me most of all one day soon, and that Dorothy would always remember her first. I read his words over and over. It seemed he was beginning to say goodbye, as I would graduate from junior high in a matter of months and our opportunities to see each other would diminish. But I also couldn't figure out what he meant by Dorothy remembering her first. Did he mean her first love, first friend, first teacher? First what?

Mom muttered away in her room, certain words emphasized more audibly almost as if she was scolding someone. Herself? Me? Dad?

My eyes returned to the Scarecrow card. I felt a pull toward him I couldn't resist and a pull toward my mother that I resented. I didn't want to be in her room with her; I wanted to be free of her. Why did it feel like I should be with her? That I should go to her? That she needed me desperately?

I sighed and groaned with irritation and she grew silent for a beat or two. Our walls were thin.

And then her muttering started up again and I repacked my suitcase and tucked it away in its secret corner. I pulled my winter coat on and fastened each button as I headed through the laundry room to the back door. I checked the exterior doorknob, unlocked as always, then stepped out on the back stoop where week-old laundry fluttered on a T-shaped clothesline Dad had strung up to save money. Down the crumbling steps, through the broken back gate, I found myself on Madison Avenue, the sidewalk riddled with purple leaves fallen from the plum trees. I slipped my hands in my coat pockets and started off down the street.

I didn't know where I'd go. I never did. Sometimes I went to the Plaza and stole food and snacks from the supermarket. Sometimes I went to neighborhood schoolyards—Taft, Roosevelt or McKinley. And sometimes, I just walked and walked until night fell and streetlamps flickered on. Occasionally I saw scary things. A man flashed me from the bushes once. Older kids huddled in dark masses at street corners. But mostly, the streets at night were empty and quiet except for the sound of my own footsteps on the pavement.

Spring of 1981
Mr. Bittle's Classroom

In first period English where I sat at the front of the class, Mr. Bittle noticed my earrings right away. I saw his eyes linger on the shiny globes on either side of my face, then a twitch, a wink and a smile.

He thought they made me look pretty, I could tell, and I took notice of being noticed. I began to style my hair more carefully, curling it back at the sides in two tidy rolls. Instead of snack food and candy, I stole cosmetics and packs of earrings, stuffing them deftly into my pockets and boldly purchasing only one or two things. I wore makeup when Dad wasn't home to see me leave the house: Baby Powder Blue eye shadow by Maybelline, super glossy Lip Smackers that smelled like bubble gum, Sweetie Pie pink blush, and Love's Baby Soft cologne. With babysitting money, I bought a pair of Jordache jeans from Ross, snug as my ballet tights but more defined around the rear end.

Mr. Bittle noticed everything, I saw it in his eyes, which first acknowledged the new accessory and then approved by way of eye contact or a wink followed by a smile. He sometimes touched my arm or my hand when no one was looking. Once, he squeezed my knee when we sat at desks beside each other. And he started talking as much as listening, treating me as a peer, not a student.

We went to public places once in a while: Mings Restaurant for an early dinner, the high school football field where we sat high in the stands and watched scrimmages and track meets, Red Morton Park with its ambling rose garden.

He told me about his family, his daughter. She was just a year or two younger than me. She went to a different school in another town and was often angry at him. I recall recognizing the similarity between his relationship with his daughter and my relationship with my dad, but as quick as the thought arrived, I rejected it. The daughter was the irrational one in his story. In my story, it was the dad who was the problem. No comparison.

Mr. Bittle also told me about his wife. She had a brain tumor and wasn't expected to survive much longer, months maybe. She rested in a hospital room, no hair, only tubes and tears. He visited her every evening and said he was tired of saying goodbye. He also said he didn't want to talk about her or his daughter when he was with me. He said I was his sanctuary, a big word for a young girl but I think I understood. I was exciting and safe at the same time, an alluring retreat.

I did not feel sad about his wife. Instead, I fantasized becoming the next Mrs. Bittle. The daughter would be a problem. I couldn't be a stepmother to a girl my own age. Perhaps she would get a brain tumor. I included this in my fantasies.

One afternoon while sitting next to one another at student desks in his empty classroom, he asked, "Do you ever think about me?"

"What do you mean? I think about you all the time," I said, feeling slightly panicked.

"But I mean, really think about me?"

His eyes stayed on mine. He inhaled deeply through his nose. His eyebrows raised a bit with angst as he confessed, "In my mind, I've made love to you thousands of times."

I looked away instantly. I was on fire, hot flames licking my skin from the inside out.

"Do you know what that means?" he asked.

"Yes, of course I do." I lied, still looking at the classroom wall to my right, covered with thumb-tacked poems and essays by students that fluttered from the breeze through the cracked windows. Maybe it meant he loved me a lot in his mind. I didn't know what "made" love meant and I also didn't understand love as something that could be quantified with numbers. If he'd loved me a thousand times, was that a lot or a little? I was confused and yet something about that phrase and the way he said it stirred something deep within, something that felt new but that I had known all along.

Spring of 1981
Across Town

One day, Mr. Bittle took me with him to help a friend move from one apartment to another. We moved boxes down steps and into the back of Mr. Bittle's blue van. His friend was older than Mr. Bittle and wore a black leather vest and a gray ponytail. He drove a motorcycle, Mr. Bittle explained, which was why we were there to help him move.

Once the van was packed, Mr. Bittle and his friend sat at the kitchen counter in the empty apartment and opened bottles of beer from the otherwise empty refrigerator. Looking at him next to his friend, I noticed that he wasn't as tall as other men and that his figure was slight, his manner more reserved. Men like his friend either leered at or completely ignored young girls like me and sometimes I couldn't quite tell the difference. But Mr. Bittle showed a regard somewhere in between, attention at arm's length. This might also have been the first time I noticed that Mr. Bittle did not have much hair. I didn't really know whether he was good-looking by social standards nor did I care. I hadn't yet learned to discriminate appearances of the opposite sex.

"Do you want one?" Mr. Bittle asked; a brown-tinted bottle extended toward me, his eyebrows raised. A twitch.

"Sure." I lied. I didn't want one actually, but I wasn't about to refuse. It tasted awful, how I imagined urine might taste. It smelled not exactly like urine but a lot like a boy's bathroom.

I left most of it untouched. But I liked pretending, my small hand wrapped around the slick bottle.

It was after dark before we left. In the passenger seat of Mr. Bittle's blue van, I began to fret about getting home so late and having to explain myself to my dad. As we approached my neighborhood I also began to worry about Mr. Bittle seeing our very messy house. These were two worlds that should not collide. I didn't see any way to avoid that, however. My dad would meet an outsider and that outsider would see inside.

Mr. Bittle pulled up to the house and suggested he walk me to the door to meet my father, and my mind froze with fear. I couldn't think of one single thing to dissuade him and I couldn't imagine what he was thinking either. Did he speculate I had a drunk for a dad or some other unacceptable childcare scenario? Was he planning to intervene in some way?

He knocked on the door and smiled down at me, confident. Twitched.

A split second later the door opened with force. Dad stepped out, grabbed my elbow, and yanked me inside.

"Go to your room now, Tamara. NOW."

I squatted in the hallway, out of sight but within earshot, my arms wrapped around my knees. I heard Mr. Bittle apologize, he was sorry it was so late, but Dad cut him short.

"Now you listen to me, Sir," he said, his voice monotone, controlled except for a slight quiver. "I've got a rifle."

There was a great pause. I heard nothing. Then Dad again.

"If I ever… catch you near my daughter again… " another great pause. "I'll use it." Silence. Then I heard the strike of the deadbolt slipping into position and I scrambled to my bed where I held my breath, heart pounding.

I didn't think about it at the time, but we never locked the doors. Our house was so lacking in proper security that the fact we'd never been robbed was the ultimate proof of its shabbiness. Not even a thief was interested in whatever was in that house. I don't know why he locked the door that night. Maybe he finally felt threatened by something. Maybe he thought locking the door would keep that world out, or me in. He never spoke to me about that night either. Not one word. Not that night, not the next morning, or anytime in the future.

June 1981
McKinley Junior High Eighth Grade Graduation

The dress I wore was too small in the bust, though I didn't notice until years later while looking at a photo. My dress was cream with red roses and in the 1970s Gunne Sax style: old-time pioneer with a touch of vintage undergarment, though no pioneer would have been seen in public in a dress with a bodice that looked like a corset. My bust had just started to blossom. I didn't even own a bra yet; I couldn't wear one with the dress anyway. It was laced up the front and pulled tightly, but not completely, closed.

Dad didn't approve at all. At our attire negotiations that morning, he grimly gave up dissent when I promised to wear a burgundy shawl the whole day. The shawl was nowhere to be seen in the photo.

After the ceremony, balloons and cheers crept skyward. Parents and their young adult children shared hugs. Mom had not come, but Dad found me and we stood opposite one another, feet apart, his hands behind his back, mine on my hips. He frowned and told me to put on my shawl. I'm sure I said something snotty. Then he left to walk home, as if he didn't even remember the incident with Mr. Bittle, who sat nonchalantly in a nearby chair with several students around him, legs outstretched, one over the other, his hands resting casually in the pockets of his Dockers.

"Congratulations, my favorite student," he said as I approached him. "You know, I'm your Scarecrow. I'm going to miss you most of all."

I looked around and bit my lower lip. My father was already out of sight.

"Would it be all right to give you a ride to the skating rink for the graduation party?"

He uncrossed his legs, bent his knees to rest his elbows on them, leaning his face into mine. "No one will see us," he assured me in almost a whisper, a very deep-voiced whisper that made my cheeks flush red and the hair on my arms rise. "No one will know. One last ride?"

"OK," I said.

As his car came to a stop in front of the low-brow building with the neon sign that commanded all who entered to SKATE, he turned off the engine and clutched the steering wheel, then breathed a slow whistle. The sun had set, the sky twilight and cool.

"Tammy, my sweet, sweet, Tammy." His hand was on my

thigh, his grip hot, large, tender but purposeful, too.

"Can I have a kiss? Just one kiss before you go?" He asked.

I set my smooth, tiny girl hand on his rough, knotty, man hand and leaned over the seat divide. He leaned toward me, face forward. I pressed my lips against his cheek lightly. He tilted his head, twitched, looked at me really strange-like, and then sat straight back up and removed his hand from my thigh and placed it back on the steering wheel.

"Okay," he said, nodding his head. "Okay."

I could see something was different, but I didn't completely understand what. He expected a different kind of kiss. He was disappointed. I didn't know how to give a different kind of kiss. If I did know how, I would have given it.

"I guess this is goodbye," he said.

"Yes, for now. I'll come back and visit you, though. All the time."

He smiled, his eyes flashed, another twitch.

"Goodbye, my Dorothy," he said.

I stepped out of his car onto the curb by the Redwood Skate entrance and stood beside the open passenger-side door. Another opportunity perhaps: If I got back in the car, what would happen? Where would we go? What would we do? I could see by his eyes that he would let me stay or let me go, whichever I chose. It would be my choice.

So much time passed. We stayed just like that, the engine running, our hearts locked in our gaze for the longest time. Was he waiting or was I?

A choice began to form, soupy at first, murky. I saw myself

getting back in his car, heading toward a destination unknown, eclipsing beyond a point of no return. My breath was caught as my mind whirled to process the shadowy fantasy: knotty hands, the soapy-musty aroma of his cheek, the smell of the boy's room, his blue eyes, my rose-patterned dress with the laced-up bodice and thin shoulder straps, the burgundy shawl I held in my hand.

But just then, he looked away toward the road ahead and I looked over my shoulder toward the skating rink. A few kids I knew milled around the entrance. When I turned back to Mr. Bittle, both hands were on his steering wheel and the trance, it seemed, was broken.

So I shut the car door and glanced at the buttery yellow moon rising between the dark buildings that formed an alley across the street. Night had come. The red roses in the pattern of my dress appeared black and I noticed that my attire had lost its softness and appeal. In the light of the moon, my graduation day gown looked stark and certain, black and white.

Mr. Bittle bent his head to see me and pressed his hand to the passenger door window. I slipped the shawl over my shoulders and pressed my hand against his through the glass. And then he drove away. Cool air tickled my fingertips as they lifted from his car. I clutched my shawl to my chest and watched as his red tail lights grew smaller and smaller until they were gone.

The Other Side of Pink

By Tambre Leighn

My mother was a perfect mother. While my father worked long hours, she spent her time shuttling my younger sister and me to ballet, birthday parties and skating lessons. Mom put up with the guinea pigs and said yes to a dog when we were old enough. She helped with homework but insisted I look spellings up on my own in the dictionary so that I would learn. And she was right—I am now an excellent speller.

Of course, life wasn't completely idyllic. There were the usual scoldings—instigated by my messy room, forgotten homework assignments, or pretending not to hear her. As I headed into my teenage years, I developed a tendency to get "lippy" as my mother put it. My tone of voice was a contentious point between us. "Oh, mother" accompanied with a tortured sigh and rolling eyes became one of my more common ways of addressing her. The older I got, the less I wanted to be like her.

When I was fourteen, my parents drove us to Montreal to

see the Summer Olympics. After a week filled with watching some of the world's best compete, my father put his three girls on a plane back home so we could start our summer skating program. Part way through the flight, the pilot announced that Hamilton was fogged in and we'd be landing in Toronto instead. My father's general manager, Rob Wright, had been designated to pick us up. Upon realizing that we'd be arriving in Toronto, an hour away from home, my mother began to worry. By the time we landed, she'd begun to whine.

"How are we supposed to get back home now? Rob won't know where we are. He won't know we're coming in late," she said helplessly.

I'd been traveling with my father since I was five years old. I had watched him negotiate us onto over-booked flights and around other obstacles.

"Don't worry, mom. They are bussing us to the Hamilton airport. I'll call the office and have Mr. Wright meet us there," I said as I put my hand out for a quarter.

It took me back to a time not long before when I had dropped a quarter in a phone booth to reach out to my mother for help. The summer I turned ten, I somehow convinced my parents to allow me to take part in a live-away skating program in St. Thomas, Ontario, several hours from home. Two other young skaters and I followed our coach there, spending nearly every waking hour studying the intricacies of balancing on the thinnest of blades while moving across the slipperiest of surfaces. The other two girls were close friends, so they shared a room.

My mom and I arrived the day before the program began.

I would be living in a school dorm with a community kitchen where we would make our meals. Together, we unpacked my things, and then headed off to Main Street. As we walked up and down the wooden floors of the St. Thomas General Store, my mother filled a shopping basket with olive green plastic plates, several cups and some cheap silverware. Off we went to the grocery store for cereal, canned soups, fresh fruit and other easily prepared items I could store in my room and a few things to be kept in the fridge with my name on them.

As the first day came to a close, I assured my mother I would be fine and she didn't have to stay overnight. She nicely, but firmly, said she was too tired to drive two hours and would stay at the Wendy Hotel that night before heading home in the morning. Around 8 p.m., she kissed me good night and tucked the card for the hotel with the phone number into my hand.

"Call me if you get lonely," she said.

I was excited to spend my first night on my own like a grown up and couldn't wait for her to leave. By 11 p.m., I was in tears. My stomach hurt and I wanted my mother. Without a roommate to distract me, I had fallen victim to my first experience of being homesick. Unable to stand the idea of being alone any longer, I called my mother. Within five minutes, she appeared outside the locked dorm doors with her hair in curlers and wrapped in her dressing gown. Her purse, dangling from her arm, looked quite out of place with the rest of her outfit. As I let her in, my tears began again.

"My stomach is upset," I told her. She put her arm around me and headed me up to my room.

"You're probably just a little scared or homesick," she said. "It's a big change being here on your own. We'll figure something out in the morning, don't worry." We curled up on the single bed and I fell quickly asleep. The next morning, my mother found a senior skater, Stephanie, who offered to let me be her roommate. All of a sudden, I was the envy of the other younger skaters. I was going to get to live with a teenager who dated boys, wore makeup and needed a bra. Stephanie showed me how to use her tiny portable record player and we sang "Band on the Run" over and over while setting up my side of the room. Later that day, my mother slipped into her two-door Chevy and pulled away smiling and waving. I wasn't sure how she'd known to stay that night but I was grateful that she had. Where had this mother gone?

I dropped the coin in the phone booth, wondering about a grown woman who couldn't figure out how to listen to the flight attendant's information and make a simple decision. My mother, who shuttled us hundreds of miles each year from ice rinks to dance studios and from the city to our summer cottage so effortlessly, couldn't make this phone call?

"Hi Taryn, it's Tambre." I explained the situation to my dad's secretary then hung up, assuring everyone that our ride home was secure. I had never seen my mom vulnerable like this before. In some ways, it scared me. When my dad arrived the next day, having driven back on his own, I proudly told him how I had handled the situation. I was, after all, my father's daughter. I knew I had stepped up and taken responsibility for my mom when she wasn't able to. I could not know this was the beginning of our family's unraveling.

Things returned to normal for a while. Mom nagged about posture and made meals with servings from all the major food groups. She overlooked the sleeping bag stuffed in the corner of my room. At some point, I had deemed making my bed a waste of precious time and the sleeping bag was my answer.

Then during tenth grade, on our spring break trip to Florida, the carefully preserved image of our family began to disintegrate. Once again, Mr. Wright was in charge of getting us to the airport on time. My father had gone down in advance on business. We loaded our bags into the company station wagon and headed toward Toronto. About ten minutes into the ride, my mother started scrounging around in her purse. At first, she was just looking. Then she became more frantic. Noticing her growing upset, I asked her what she was looking for.

"My pills. I can't find my pills," she said with a touch of panic in her voice. She looked up. "We have to turn around and go back."

"We can't." I insisted. "We'll miss the flight. They're probably in your carry on."

"Well, you have to check," she demanded, her voice rising in pitch with each new piece of dialogue.

I looked into the back and discovered the carry on was buried deep under our larger suitcases. When I let her know I couldn't reach it, she went into a full panic that turned into an argument. At one point, Mr. Wright asked weakly if she really wanted to turn around but I overrode him, insisting we would miss the flight. I had no idea how vulnerable the thought of being without her medication made her feel in that moment.

I wouldn't know for another several years that she had become addicted to her prescribed anti-anxiety medication and without it she was lost. Somehow, I won and we traveled the rest of the way in silence. When we arrived, she bolted from the car and hauled her carry on from the back. She popped it open so quickly, the contents spilled onto the ground. My mother desperately scrambled around in the gutter to gather up the brown plastic bottles that were her lifeline.

I choked back the feeling of disgust as I helped her close up the case, her precious cargo once again back inside. I tried to dispel the image of her shaking hands grasping at the bottles. Instead, I wanted to remember my most perfect picture of her, dressed like Cinderella six years before as she and my father headed out to a fundraising ball. That night, she stood before my sister and me in a slender evening gown made of the softest cotton candy color. A tiny jacket striped with soft greens and fringed with a collar of pink boa feathers wrapped around her bone thin shoulders. Her perfectly blonde dyed hair was her crown. What had become of the fairytale princess? Though my family seemed to be perfect, cracks and fissures were beginning to appear.

By the time I was sixteen, my mother spent most of her days riding her prescription pills to the highs, then crashing into drug induced slumbers. My weekdays involved typical high school things: attending classes, participating in gymnastics and various other school activities. But my nights and weekends were often far from normal. Sometimes I would arrive home from school and find my mother sitting on the couch, dressed with her hair brushed.

"Hi, honey, how was your day?" She'd ask, just like when I was in middle school. I'd plop down in the gold corduroy chair and count my blessings as I shared the goings on with her. I never allowed myself to hope that every day would be like this. She was just as inclined to greet me at the door needing to argue, her confidence boosted artificially by the drugs. Even if I had told her I'd be home late because of a practice or after school meeting, I could find myself walking into a battlefield.

"Just what the hell were you up to when you know I'm stuck here at home sick? I need you to be here for me," she'd scream.

I would do my best to diffuse her rage.

"Remember, I told you I had gymnastics practice," I said, begging her to recall there was no need for her to be angry.

"Go ahead and be selfish, then. Leave me here to take care of your sister when you know I'm not well." And I did feel selfish for making even the smallest attempt to maintain a normal life. Some days, I was successful and could get her to settle down. Usually heading directly to the kitchen to prepare dinner would help. But other times I didn't have the tools to talk reason to the drugs and on those days I resorted to the pager. For the last two years of my mother's life, my father wore one everywhere he went. When I could not control my mother, I would page him a 911 and he would drop what he was doing to come home and intervene.

During the final month of school in eleventh grade, her depression seemed to escalate and she spent weeks in bed. I spent so much time caring for her that I hadn't found the opportunity to shop for the upcoming formal. On the last

Saturday morning before the big day, I sat down next to my father at the breakfast table. Mom was, as usual, still in bed.

I hated to ask. "You know, dad, the formal is next Thursday night and I don't have a dress yet." It wasn't just the dress that I wanted. It was what the other girls in class had that meant more to me. This was the day they were jumping into cars with their mothers and heading off to find the perfect gown and matching shoes. They would be celebrating with a special lunch and choosing nail polish colors together.

My dad reached into his pocket and pulled out folded bills.

"I'll cover for you this morning. You go out and get something beautiful to wear," he said with sadness in his eyes.

I swallowed hard as he peeled off hundred dollar bills and folded them into my hand. Quietly, I snuck out and headed to the mall. When I got home several hours later, my mother called to me from her bed.

"Where have you been?"

"She was doing some errands for me, Lenore," my father said so I didn't have to lie. To tell her I'd been shopping for my formal would have induced yet another lecture on my acute selfishness. I recall hiding the dress until the day before and then trying to bring only the slightest attention to its unveiling.

"Isn't tomorrow night the formal?" she asked, nearly a week later. "What are you going to wear?"

I went to my closet and lifted the hanger. I had been surprised at my choice. It was a color I never wore. I walked into my mother's room and held it up in front of me.

"That pink will look lovely on you," she said in a voice full of regret for the moment we both knew she had missed.

Stiff Competition

By Thomas Burke

My friend Tom had a tape in with his cassettes that casually sat right next to the Fine Young Cannibals and UB40. The title of the tape was handwritten— *For Thomas, My Love*—by his mom in blue marker.

I wanted that tape, badly. Whenever I was over at his house and Tom was in the bathroom or talking with his dad, I'd want to slip it in the deck for a quick listen, or "borrow" it and stick Funky Cold Medina in its case until I brought it back; I even considered outright stealing it and just playing dumb if he ever questioned me.

With everything we did back then—all the shared hideousness and stupidity—I never grew enough of that particular sort of pluck to invade that space of his. If anything was sacred back then, and, admittedly, very, *very* little was, the relationship between Tom and his mom took that title.

That being said, my best friend Tom and I were two irreverent, nearly-irreproachable misfits—fourth graders who lived like pint-sized and carefree merchant marines on weekend passes, always willing and always able to find something to stick our winkies in, metaphorically speaking. When we did things it was with little or no remorse; even then, we had a waning sense of morality.

We were the kids from down the street that mowed your lawn for five bucks; we were the small-framed lads in the park smoking pipes of cherry Cavendish; we threw ninja stars at squirrels; and we were the townies that rode around Northwestern University's campus yelling at coeds and stealing hood ornaments. We were mildly masochistic, substantially sadistic preteens with burgeoning, though powerful, sexual appetites.

We never really got caught doing anything, and even when we did, we were still prim and proper in the adults' eyes; we would blink a tear, apologize, and go back to being like bleached sheets drying on the line. I suppose we flew below the radar of unmistakably demented behavior. Other people in our school consistently drew the attention of our superiors from us.

Joyce McCoy, for example, was one of the least grounded people I have ever known; she was the type of child authorities kept their eye on. Occasionally Joyce would work the ropes during one of my failed attempts at double dutch jump roping, but in the fifth grade, I knew Joyce best from sitting next to her in social studies—we were both in the last row by the windows, next to the radiators. In the winter, our school's furnace would crank heat throughout the school, such that Mrs. Fischer—who was maybe juggling the early stages of menopause, forever talking about the temperature—made us keep the windows open.

So while Joyce and I watched snow drifts form on our textbooks and listened to Mrs. Fischer interrupt lessons with her "Aren't all of you hot? My, it certainly is hot in here…" Joyce would take the ring off her finger and put it on the radiator, using the heat source like it was cast-iron hibachi. She had amazing patience, Joyce did, and she'd let it cook for almost an entire period. Then, in the middle of one of Mrs. Fischer's sentences, she'd take two pens in her hand like chopsticks, pick up the suspiciously cool-looking ring, and drop it down the shirt collar of the poor, unsuspecting boy in front of her, who'd end up with circular third degree burns from his neck to the small of his back.

Joyce McCoy ended up in a juvee home because of a stunt she pulled the summer after fifth grade. She stole a school bus and drove across Howard Street into Chicago. She was tiny, and because she couldn't see to steer and press the accelerator at the same time, she crashed into a streetlight. That was brass, beyond our scope.

Even though Joyce was small, she could beat up all the boys, all of them except Bradley Jones, who was big and mature—he had a mustache when we left elementary school. Bradley said he'd had sex with Joyce in the boy's room in the fifth grade—a story he recounted to our gym class in the locker room on several occasions while we changed into our polyester shorts and flung heavy, wet paper towel balls at each other.

Sex for Tom and me, in the fifth grade, wasn't quite a reality. It wasn't for lack of an entire library of videos and magazines at our disposal, to teach us. But we definitely weren't getting any real action, not like Bradley was.

Tom and I spent a lot of time with a buddy of ours, Matt, who lived near us. Matt's dad had a taste for pornography, which was great because Tom, Matt, and I did too. Tom and I spent, I would guess, well over half of our fifth grade afternoons at Matt's perusing movies and comparing raunchy letters to the editors.

Both of Matt's parents were lawyers and worked late. Babysitters never lasted long, never spoke English very well, were always afraid of Matt's misanthropic older brother and the family's neglected golden retriever; basically, we had a house to ourselves to learn about sex.

Assumptions about sex when I was in the fifth grade: it is unlikely, but possible, that if you order an extra large super bell pepper pizza, it will be delivered on roller skates by an eighteen-year-old blond in short shorts and a tank top who will be happy to provide oral sex before she is sodomized. It's unlikely, but possible, that there are pay-per-view competitions where two women go to opposite ends of a boxing ring and have a blow job competition to see who can make the man ejaculate first. Sure, we knew characters like Cynthia Silk Throat and Tammy the Tongue were just bits from a movie, but what if? If there was, surely the Don Kings of the industry would always be on the lookout for men willing to provide the apparatus for these women to compete with.

Exposure to such things made chronic masturbation a necessity, so I set up a little chamber in my closet in the fifth grade. It was crude, but one of the only personal spaces

I could find; I shared a bathroom with my mom and the lock didn't work. The closet was cozy—I had a soft cotton blanket sprawled on the floor—and I'd climb underneath my blazer and my parents' nonessential garments, pick a season from my Victoria's Secret catalog collection, depress three or four portions of intensive care lotion in my hand, and go to town. For the amount of time I spent in that closet, who knows what my parents must have thought. I haven't yet asked their opinion in my search for insight in this matter.

I didn't get my first kiss until a year later and—even though we were in, or at least on the fringes, of the popular crowd—Tom and I didn't get much attention from the ladies. We were nothing special to look at: two pudgy, pasty kids with almost-cool hand me down t-shirts from our brothers and French-rolls on the cuffs of our jeans. We both had buzz cuts, Tom's accented with long, skater bangs that he sometimes crimped, mine with a mouth full of steel correcting my gnarled smile, the result of an upside-down, backwards bicuspid.

Even though we weren't paid much attention to didn't mean we didn't pine over the girls to no end. We got to the point of writing our favorite young ladies in our class anonymous love letters. Love letters? Probably those girls, even today, wouldn't consider any part of them romantic.

We used a typewriter to maintain anonymity, and our recently acquired expertise on talking sexy to women, vis-à-vis the XXX, to woo them. They were full of "I want to press your… and stick my… I want to shoot… grab handfuls of your hair… lots of foreplay before… want to eat…" And each letter ended, "Please don't show this to *anyone* because then I'll be too embarrassed to tell you who I am. Love always, your secret admirer."

We thought it was great, wrote to six or seven different girls, staying after the bell to stick the envelopes through the ventilation slots in their lockers. Twice, before class started and in our presence, blushing girls meekly handed letters over to Mrs. Fischer saying that their moms had asked that they show them to her. Mrs. Fischer read the letters while she wiped the sweat off her forehead and neck with a handkerchief, but she never made anything of them. Those letters might have been a bit explicit for her to deal with, a bit too visual for our innocent classmates.

Mrs. Fischer and I had a decent relationship—I think she liked me, despite my lack of motivation. Starting with the first month of the fifth grade, I decided that I wasn't going to do any homework. I didn't do a single assignment in any class. There was a chart on the wall of Mrs. Fischer's classroom that was supposed to help us monitor our missing assignments, and my column was empty. I got to the point of simply avoiding that part of the room, throwing out garbage in the hallway instead of using the trash bin on the carpet just under that looming poster board.

It's easy to not do homework, but consistently avoiding homework responsibilities is work in itself. After school, instead of hitting the books like we'd promised Mrs. Fischer we'd do, Tom, Matt, and I would go over to Matt's house and feed our brains on *The Confessions of a Teenage Nymphomaniac* or *Hot and Saucy Pizza Girls*.

We devised ways to cheat on tests. Like on spelling quizzes:

we'd write the required list on a piece of paper, pressing our ball point pens down hard so that they embossed the sheet underneath it. We handcrafted elaborate crib sheets for math class and history tests. Sometimes we took notes down in light pencil on our enamel desktops, licking our fingers and smearing the evidence away as soon as we passed in our papers.

Sometimes when I wasn't doing homework, my brother Alex taught me about claustrophobia, that feeling of helplessness that accompanies being pinned or confined against your will, sometimes for long periods of time. I'd squirm and kick my legs to try and free myself from Alex's grip, but with those three years he had on me, he was always too big for me to contend with.

One time he and a friend were playing Atari in our family room, and I sat down on the floor to watch. I suppose their heated session of shuffle puck wasn't engrossing enough, because they turned their attention to me. As per the normal sequence of events, they pinned me down and roughed me up a bit. Then they got creative. They were thinking in terms of TV's inventive, never-at-a-loss icon MacGyver: What've we got? This old blanket, that couch, a television, the Atari, and a kid? They unfolded a thick, scratchy blanket, put me horizontally at one end—one of them pulled my legs straight while the other yanked my arms up over my head—and rolled me up like a tight cigar. They tore the cushions off the couch, tossed me onto the loose change and gum wrappers, piled the cushions back into place, sat on top of me, and idly resumed their game of shuffle puck with a screaming, hyperventilating kid underneath them.

I wasn't always a pushover. I was a fighter, got scrappier after each torture session. Like after the couch incident; later that same day my brother was picking on me on the front lawn. I was pinned down—his knees on top of both my wrists and shoulders at once—and he was flicking my ears so that they stung. He was dripping a thick stream of mucus-infused saliva from his mouth towards my face and slurping it back up before it filled my eye socket. Incidentally, he's let it drop on a few occasions. Frustrated, I did the only thing I could—I opened my mouth, heaved my face at his crotch, and bit what I caught between my teeth for all I was worth.

He wailed, shrieked, screamed bloody murder, hopped off me, and ran around the yard like he was possessed. I was oddly satisfied. My mom, at the shrieks, ran out the front door to see what the matter was. She took my brother inside and made him show her the marks, I guess to see if he needed to go to the hospital. He didn't.

My parents scolded me. Alex was disgusted, kept asking me how I could conceive of doing something so horrific, how I could not understand the unspoken off-limits always respected during male to male combat. It was an awkward feeling, but I knew it'd be a little while before he did anything to me again. And it was. Not forever, but for a short time; at least, I suppose, until he was no longer reminded of my inner strength every time he peed.

As much as Alex beat the hell out of me, he was still my older brother and had brotherly duties. He protected me from a bully once, said he'd take care of him, and did. As fate would have it though, years later I made friends with that bully in high school; he died about a month after our re-acquaintance, when he was a senior in high school, during a drunken drag race gone horribly sour.

On another occasion, Halloween in the fifth grade, Tom and I—dressed as Bob and Doug McKenzie from the TV show *SCTV* and the movie *Strange Brew*—were confronted on the street by six older boys. These guys were dressed, very convincingly, as thugs: ski masks, baseball bats, dark shirts, lengths of iron chains, sawed off broomsticks with grip tape on the handles. They circled us and pulled us off the sidewalk into the walkway between two houses, and told us they wanted our heavy pillowcases full of candy. We whimpered and pleaded, like pussycats, but then one of the guys said, "Hey, that's Alex's little brother. Hey, kid, we were just messing with you. We don't really want your candy."

Tom's older brother, Franz, was the same age as Alex, but none of those guys recognized Tom as anyone's younger sibling. Not that Alex would have necessarily been roughing up youngsters—other than me—for candy, but I guess he had a wider ring of friends than Franz, was less constricted. Franz had a different relationship with Tom, was in a much different place.

Rita died on Sunday at Evanston Hospital after a five-year battle with cancer. She is survived by her loving family: her husband, Eberhard, a German chemist who teaches at Northwestern University; her sons, Franz- a 7th grader at Haven Middle School, Thomas- a 4th grader at Orrington School; and her daughter, Catherine- a 1st grader at Orrington School. Services will be...

Tom's family lived near Evanston Hospital, which has

one of the best cancer treatment centers in the world—the place his mom died the year before. His house, to be exact, was directly across the street from the automobile entrance to the emergency room. One day during winter break from fifth grade, Tom and I decided to make a snow fort on his front lawn so we could throw snowballs at passing cars. The hospital entrance was on a busy street, which meant lots of moving targets; and because the emergency room was right there, cars would slow down and sometimes stop while they were turning in, and we'd nail them.

We made about a hundred ice balls and started flinging the things at every car that passed. It wasn't the brightest plan, as our fort concealed nothing but our faces. But "TNT" had a blast with all the ducking down, the laughing, and the high fives. It was great, until an oversized sedan that we'd pegged with almost a dozen ice balls stopped just after turning into the hospital's driveway. An old man in a ragged fox fur cap jumped out, stormed at us, stomped down our fort, and told us his wife was very sick and that we ought to be ashamed of ourselves. He asked whether the house we were in front of was ours? "Uh, no. We live a few blocks down and towards the lake." He mumbled something, then ran back across the street and gunned it towards the emergency room.

We ran off, and in case the old man came back to get us, we doubled back through the alley and hid out in the crawlspace under Tom's porch with their black lab, Shadow, picking through the hay bail insulation that made Shadow's home.

When we went into the house, Franz was watching television, and he was excited to hear the details as they poured out. Franz was very kind. Alex would never have been as anxious to know about our little accomplishments, but Franz, he was the supportive older brother; a few years later, he'd be the one to buy us beer until we got fake IDs.

Sometimes we'd hang out with Franz like he was one of us, and he never let on that he was embarrassed to be with guys three years younger. Franz was cool because he had nunchucks, a samurai sword, throwing darts, *Soldier of Fortune* catalogs, a collection of hatchets, BB guns, and sixteen inch survival knives that he'd let us play with. He would demonstrate how to properly throw a ninja star at a target, which was often a picture of a supermodel taken from a fashion magazine that was stuck into a tree with a buck knife.

A live animal had a fifty-fifty chance of survival if it found its way into the backyard during a target practice. If the thing lived, it wouldn't have been because of a lack of effort.

Franz was the one who showed us the pleasures of riding our bikes through the Northwestern University campus. For some reason, many of the buildings on campus—the ugly ones that were postmodern at some time—were constructed with long, steep ramps instead of stairs: perfect for fearless preteens to rush down, fun for weaving in and out of daydreaming college students on, great for whipping around blind corners and nearly colliding with pedestrians at reckless speeds.

But it was peaceful there, too. The landfill extends the campus out into Lake Michigan, and there's a bike path following the shore that we'd ride on when the weather was nice. Once, Tom, Franz, and I were taking a breather on the boulders that made the landfill's breakwater, looking out on the lake—sitting, as we always did, next to the rock with the painting of a naked, well-proportioned woman on it—and some older kids from school rode over and took Tom's and mine's bicycles. Tom and I looked immediately to Franz, and he had this helpless expression on his face. But he got on his bike and pedaled after them. Tom and I ran to catch up.

When we got to where Franz had caught up with the three guys, they were calling Franz a stupid, white mother fucker. The tension was foreign to me, and to Tom, too. Franz just kept asking for the bikes back, angry but scared. "Just give them their bikes, man. Just give them back." One of the guys unfolded the blade on a small Victorinox pocketknife and said, "Take your fucking bikes, white boy." Then they got on their own bikes and rode off.

None of us said anything, just started riding home. Franz, though, began to sob, and then he became enraged. "Man, those fucking niggers." It was the first time I'd ever heard someone use the word nigger. He was grimacing, crying, shaking his head back and forth, standing straight up on his pedals and riding hard. "Those fucking niggers, man. Those fucking niggers. Why the fuck do they have to do that?" Tom tried to say something encouraging and loving to his brother, but Franz was inconsolable. I was confused, and at the time I chalked Franz's racism up to his German background—the asinine notion that all Germans still had some genetically unalterable Third Reich tendencies.

Franz sometimes hung out with Michael, Matt's older brother. Michael was the misanthrope babysitters feared. We feared him too, but in a different way. We feared him for his strangeness. Michael hated his parents. He would walk around the house spitting on the carpet and cursing wildly as he rubbed in the wet spots with his heavy combat boots. He'd barge into our porn viewings, unwrap one of his dad's condoms, blow it up like a balloon, then forcefully, though awkwardly rub it all over Matt's face and mouth until one of the metal edges of Matt's braces would pop it. He'd expound on the affairs of the government, call us faggots, sometimes he'd kick their dog, Kate, in the head, and other times he'd wiggle around on the carpet with her like they were lovers.

But Matt, and especially Michael, had it bad in that household. Their dad was a large man, with a huge, swollen belly, and he intimidated with his size, voice, and diction. He treated us like we weren't kids.

Matt had a sleepover birthday party in the fifth grade. Tom and I were there, Michael invited Franz so he'd have a friend, and Matt made the gutsy move of inviting five or six boys from a slightly higher social echelon to join us. The party was fun, pizza and basketball, and as the night got later, we hyped ourselves up on Jolt Cola and Now and Laters to prepare for the eight hours of movies we'd rented. After *The Goonies* and *Revenge of the Nerds*, at about midnight, we started flipping through the cable channels. Late night Cinemax was showing an interesting film. It was softcore porn, lighter than the stuff we were used to, but still pretty good.

A naked man had lifted and was holding a naked woman up his arms—a kind of backwards piggyback ride—and they were doing it that way when Matt's dad barged into the room. "Jesus Christ. All right, Matt, give me my goddamned videotape." Ten pale faces shot back and forth between Matt and his dad.

"It's not your tape, Dad. See? It's not a tape." Matt pressed eject on the VCR and the tape chamber popped up empty. "See Dad, it's on TV."

"Jesus fucking Christ." And Matt's dad left, slamming the door behind him, and leaving us to continue our research on typical sexual positions.

I'll admit though, that what confused me the most at the time—what was the most disconcerting about the situation— was that Matt's dad didn't recognize that the movie wasn't from his library. I would have known, right away, that it wasn't; I knew almost every scene of every movie he owned.

Matt's dad had a long cherry red '68 Chevy convertible that he loved to drive us around in with the top down, that is, on the few occasions that he did. He took Matt, Michael, Tom, and me out to dinner in that car once in the fifth grade, and I knew from the beginning that the night was going to end badly, even before we left. We were all in the driveway, sitting in the car waiting for Michael, and his dad became impatient. He honked the horn repeatedly, obnoxiously. Then he yelled at the house, as loud as he could. "Michael! Get your fat fucking ass down here! You've had time to jerk off three times and take a shower! Now get the fuck in this car!"

When we got back from the restaurant, Michael immediately hopped on his bike and took off, and Tom, Matt, and I went up to the third floor to where Michael's and Matt's bedrooms were. As we often did, especially when we knew he wouldn't be back for some time, we began to snoop through

Michael's stuff. Matt's dad yelled for Matt to go downstairs, and when he did, Tom and I found a *Penthouse* under a pile of Michael's dirty laundry.

It pleased us, held our attention, got us to mill around for ten minutes and drool like morons, anyway. But when we got to the centerfold, the pages had been plastered together with the dried remains of one of Michael's pleasure sessions. So Tom and I, knowing full well the brilliance and rarity of such a revolting item, decided to put it to use.

When Matt came back up, I got on the weightlifting bench and pretended that I was too weak to bench press the bar with no weights on it. I struggled, swore that the steel was too damn heavy. Just as I'd hoped, Matt started to taunt me.

"You can't lift that? You pussy."

"Let's see you do it. You can't do it; this fucking thing is *heavy*."

"Get out of the way."

Matt started to bench press the bar, over and over, very quickly, laughing, smirking, reminding me what a weakling I was. But that's when I bent over him and put all my weight on the bar, on his chest, holding him firmly in place. Then Tom came in from the other room, flipped the magazine to the soiled centerfold, and rubbed it all over his face. Then the two of us bolted, lunged down the stairs, busted out the front door and ran all the way to Tom's house. As we twisted around the banister at the third floor landing, we could hear Matt piecing things together: "What the…? Huh? Oh, God!"

Matt's dad called Tom's house ten minutes later, and even though the receiver was to Tom's ear, I could still hear the strings of profanity and disgust being dealt our way. "What an asshole," Tom and I giggled after he hung up the phone. But we did still feel badly, for Matt.

We went on a school field trip in the fifth grade to Camp Timberlee—a Christian camp in the summer, mostly secular for our purposes—for a week of outdoor adventure and bonding.

It was raining on our fourth day at Camp Timberlee. A group of us were walking to dinner, and we were being smart asses. "Mudder Fudder" we were saying. "That guy's a mudder fudder! Mudder fudder, mudder fudder, mudder fudder!" Then I got bold and said, loud enough for the entire group to hear, "It's not mudder fudder, it's mother fucker, you mother fuckers!"

One of the Bible beaters who'd facilitated our trust walk that afternoon came over to us. "Who said that?" I was feeling some mettle, proud that I'd said what others had been afraid to, so I answered quickly and directly. "I did." The man took me firmly by the collar and marched me to a bench. He sat me down, then sat himself next to me. There we were, sitting in the rain without coats or ponchos, and he began his speech, which I have no doubt he believed would change my life. His voice and demeanor suggested that his words would have that kind of effect.

"What you said back there, that's a nasty thing to say. A really nasty, devilish thing."

"I know."

"Do you know what kind of creature says that kind of word? Do you?"

"No."

"Rats."

"Yeah?"

"Yes. Rats. Rats use that kind of language. And do you know where rats live?"

"Where?"

"Rats live in the sewer. Rats are dirty, dirty creatures, they live in the sewer, and they use that kind of language."

"Oh."

"Are you a rat?"

"No?"

"Do you want to be a rat? Do you want to live in the sewer?"

"No."

"So are you going to ever use that kind of language again? Are you going to live like a rat?"

"No. I don't want to be a rat."

"That's good. Very good." Then he gave me a few pats on the back and sent me to the dining hall.

Seven words continuously resurfaced in my vocabulary over the next week, two of them more than the others: mudder, fudder, dirty, sewer, rat, mother, and fucker. I doubt that that counselor had any idea that his thoughtful discourse would turn into an excuse to curse even more.

The week before spring break, Tom and I got into a nasty fight. I was jealous of Tom, at that time, because he was going with Matt's family to Sanibel Island for spring vacation, and I was stuck going to a family reunion in southeastern Indiana.

That Wednesday after school, Tom, Matt, and I were walking around our neighborhood bouncing a basketball and telling jokes with two girls—tomboys we'd grown up with, though they were on the verge of becoming gorgeous.

Somewhere along the way, I made a crack about Tom's penis: "What's up with that Tic Tac dick of yours, man?" Of course we all had Tic Tacs, relatively speaking, since our only exposure to the standard size of mature penises was through the donkey dong lens of *Stiff Competition* and *Learning to Ride—the Hard Way*.

So I threw out the insult, we laughed, the girls giggled and whispered to each other, and Tom picked up the basketball and flung it at me. He missed, and the ball sailed across the street and into some bushes. Matt yelled at Tom to go and get his basketball, and I made a few more comments about Tom's penis while he was gone. Then, while I swaggered and chuckled, the basketball was suddenly bouncing off the side of my face, and my eardrum started to buzz, moan, then squeal like a siren.

There was a brief round of catch the wild turkey, but I managed to snag the back of his shirt with some of my fingers. I stopped him, put one hand on his waist and the other on his shoulder, and threw him to the ground as hard as I could. I got on top of him, and just before I started pounding, I stopped. I gave him a speech instead, talked about how I didn't want to hurt him because he was my friend, that friends don't do that to each other. With the super-fuel of my self-righteousness, I didn't punch him even once.

But while I hovered over Tom and delivered my soliloquy,

he was cringing, holding his shoulder, crying. I had this bad feeling Tom was really hurt. It turned out I'd broken his collarbone, and he spent his week on Sanibel Island with a big white air cast strapped around his torso, his arm completely immobilized. He wasn't allowed to swim in the ocean, never mind those tan lines.

Meanwhile, I was in Indiana with my relatives. One night of that week, we were all in my grandparent's hotel room, the adults drinking and the kids doing very little. I was watching my grandmother as she sat on the comforter, maudlin and smiling with her plastic cup of raspberry schnapps, so happy to be surrounded by her children and so many grandchildren.

My Uncle Ted, a geography professor at Northern Kentucky, came up to me that night and asked me about school. Uncle Ted was the kind of guy who wanted real answers, not the "fine" or "all right" that worked with some of the others. I was savvy enough to know that a vivid description of how I'd done zero homework for half a year wouldn't have gone over too well, so I said that I liked all my classes.

"And what subject do you like the most?"

I thought about it, and told him it was writing, which was true.

"How about you write something for me? Would you be willing to do that?" I said sure, and he walked over to the bedside table, picked up a Four Winds pen and a Four Winds pad of paper, and handed them to me. I knelt down on the floor, used the bed as a desk, and started writing.

Freddy Krueger... his victim on a table... got a sharpening stone... knives on his gloves sparkled... scratched his name in the mirror… cut her up…blood on his sweater… sliced her to pieces… she screamed a lot… he liked his work.

"Well, Tom, this is a fairly unique style." Then Uncle Ted laughed out loud. He walked over to my dad and showed the story to him. My dad laughed too, but I think he was embarrassed or concerned, and maybe he ought to have been both. All three of us decided it was best not to show Grandmother how I'd developed my writing up to that point.

When the school year ended—at about the same time Joyce McCoy was giving herself her first driving lesson—Tom, Matt, and I went on a YMCA camping trip together. We spent a week in the Upper Peninsula of Michigan hiking the North Country trail and canoeing the Big Two Hearted River.

What was so special about this trip was that we had an independence that we hadn't known before. Sure, Ish and Walsh, our twenty-five year old counselors, were there to supervise, but they mentored more than disciplined. We finally had role models that were fun and cool, kind and realistic, physical but gentle, crass but dependable, shameless and honest, and completely accessible. The most important thing we took from that trip was that we were normal: our desires, dreams, faults, and peculiar interests weren't strange. For a week, Tom, Matt, and I had loving older brothers, two of them. And we were good friends, weren't thinking about anything but how damn nice it was just then.

Tom fell in love with that feeling the most; he fell for Ish and Walsh like they were some kind of narcotic.

Walsh had a weenie/marshmallow stick that he toted on his pack and in his canoe for the entire trip. At our last campfire, Walsh presented it to Tom as a kind of award for wrapping his canoe around a rock in one of the lazy rapids. Tom ran around the fire like a crazy man, and the heat of the flames seemed to harden an epoxy around his grin.

Part way back home to Evanston, our group merged with the kids who'd stayed in Central Michigan at the main camp. Tom took his stick with him to his seat, for safekeeping, and I sat next to him, on the aisle. About ten minutes into the ride, the junior counselor working on our bus came back to check on things. When he saw the long stick resting between us, and before we could say anything, he grabbed it, and broke it in half, then into quarters. "Sorry guy, no sticks on the bus."

It would be impossible to duplicate the sound that came out of Tom's mouth—it was a cross between a pubescent choirboy doing vocal warm-ups and the noise a little girl would make if she was getting punched hard in the stomach. The counselor knew immediately that he'd done something awful, and I could see the regret, the shock, and the what-in-the-world-do-I-do-now look on his face. Even so, Tom hated him, and I hated him, too.

To his credit, the counselor demonstrated how the stick was more useful now as a tool to poke people with two rows up on the bus. That softened the blow, but the swing had already connected.

"I'm sorry," the counselor said. "I had no idea. I'm really, really sorry."

Tom just stared out the window, didn't bother to wipe his cheeks of the steady flow from his eyes.

"It's all right, man." I said to Tom. "The stick may be

broken, but that doesn't change anything about our trip. It's just a stick anyway, right?"

Tom shrugged his shoulders, but kept his head against the glass, his eyes watching the cornfields.

"It'll be all right," I repeated. "It's just a stick, man."

For the rest of the trip home, I thought about the tape Tom's mom had made him. I imagined that his mom had anticipated the situations that Tom would need a mother's love, and spoken into a microphone about them. Maybe, instead of a song list on the tape's insert, Tom's mom had written down which part of the tape to listen to at certain times in his life: minute seventeen, *a tip for your first date*; minute twenty-nine, *for when you get sick*; minute thirty, *advice for when you lose something dear to you*; minute thirty-nine, *something for when you get lonely*; minute forty-three, *the happy birthday song*.

I still have no idea what's on that tape. I've always hoped it held, among other things, the secrets of the world and an answer to the question of life. I used to think of the tape as a physical replacement for a person, his mom reincarnated into clear plastic; that idea was as stupid as it was genuine.

I figure that at the very least, Tom has a recording of his mom's voice saying she loves him more than he could know, and in some ways I don't know how much more he'd really want. I really don't know.

When the buses pulled into the YMCA's parking lot in Evanston, our parents were there waiting. I was showered with hugs that made me feel young and smothered and loved. Matt got hugs too, and he looked relieved to be back. As for Tom, he held on to his dad for a long time, crying into his dad's chest. We were still young boys, despite all we had or hadn't done and seen.

Chalk

By Anthony D'Aries

Billy Baker lived down the street from me, near the dead end. I was ten and he was eight, but he had a way about him that made him seem older. He lived with his mother and two sisters, Maggie, eleven, the oldest, and Josephina, five. His father showed up every other week or so. We could hear the music blasting from his white Camaro as he pulled around the corner. He parked in the street, wheels angled toward the road. I remember him walking across the front lawn—a tall thin man with short dark curly hair, white sweater, black jeans and tennis shoes. He stopped to pick up a bright yellow Tonka truck off the lawn and carry it to the front of the house.

"Hiya, Bill," he said, dropping the truck in the patch of dirt beneath the front windows. There was no garden, no bushes in front of his house like mine, no tall flowers or pine trees—only a strip of dirt and a chipped gray foundation.

Billy and I sat on the front steps, crushing small rocks with larger rocks. His dad slid his iridescent sunglasses into his hair and squeezed the back of Billy's neck. He called me "Tony," the only one who used that nickname, and it always made me feel like he knew some secret about me. I smiled politely as he walked past us and into the house.

The inside of Billy's house was like a wound, something delicate ripped wide open. Josephina's juice boxes and melted ice pops left hard red blotches on the beige carpet. Crushed saltine crackers dusted the stairs. The big red couch was stained with Coca-Cola and one of the cushions was torn so badly it looked like it was sliced with a steak knife. When we watched TV, Billy pulled chunks of cotton from the couch and threw them on the floor. Billy's father didn't seem to notice.

His father walked down the hall and into the bedroom. I heard him say something to Billy's mother and shut the door behind him. Billy nudged me with his elbow, thin black hairs curling over his top lip as he grinned. He muted the television and crept toward the hallway. Maggie sat with perfect posture at the kitchen table behind a fort of math and science textbooks covered with brown paper bags. Josephina was alone with her bucket of chalk in the driveway. Billy beckoned me toward the hallway.

We got down on our hands and knees and crawled toward the bedroom door. I was right behind Billy, the black bottoms of his bare feet inches away from the tips of my fingers. He turned around and slid backwards on his butt until his back was against the wall. I crawled forward and sat next to him. Billy put his finger to his lips.

His mother moaned—a soft whimpering, the whispers of a foreign language. Steady and breathy, as if there wasn't enough air in her bedroom. Billy giggled quietly, thrusting his hips into the air. I'd heard these sounds in the movies Billy and I watched on cable late at night, men and women rolling in bed with sweaty, painful expressions, but I had never heard them in real life. She moaned louder; I pressed my ear to the door.

"Billy!" Maggie whispered, peeking over her thick textbook. "Get away from there."

Billy looked at her, gave her the finger. She shook her head and looked at me. I shook my head, too, with half a smile as if I didn't want to believe what was happening. Part of me didn't. Part of me was frightened of what went on inside their house. The other part was curious.

Her moans quickened and for the first time I heard the bass of his father's voice, then silence. Normal sounds slowly broke through the blood-rush in my ears—the scratching of Maggie's pencil, Josephina's singing in the driveway, the cool outside air blowing through the curtains. The bed creaked, and we ran back to the living room.

A few minutes later, his father came out of the bedroom and walked into the kitchen. He stretched in front of the open refrigerator with a can of Diet Coke in his hand. He popped the top and took a long swallow; each gulp audible in his throat. I pretended to watch TV as I stared at him leaning on the refrigerator door, absently flipping through a stack of Josephina's drawings stuck to the freezer with magnets shaped like fruits and vegetables. He held up a family portrait—the mother in a long bathrobe with wild hair, Maggie standing up straight, neat clothes, arms full of books, Billy holding a toy gun, spraying bullets in the air like a cowboy, and the father smiling in his white Camaro, three lines shooting out from the back of the car to show how fast he was going.

He put the portrait back on the freezer and finished his Diet Coke. The delicate echo of the empty can on the counter followed by the papery slap of an envelope filled with money. He kissed Maggie on the cheek and walked into the living room, said goodbye to me and Billy, took a quick look around the house, put his sunglasses on and closed the door. We heard him whistle as he walked across the front lawn. Through the window, I watched him get in his car, the convertible top blossoming as he drove up the street.

Billy's mother shuffled out of the bedroom, her bathrobe never completely closed, always revealing too much: a blotchy breast, a pale veiny thigh. She seemed to sleepwalk everywhere she went—the kitchen, the backyard, the elementary school to pick up Josephina. In the evenings, Billy forced her to walk to McDonald's and get us food. Screaming and cursing, he told her to get a pen and write down our order. He said it was okay, that I could go ahead and tell her what I wanted. She knelt beside me with a pen in her hand, looking up at me with exhaustion, as if my answer could save her. I told her what I wanted.

As chaotic as Billy's house was, I didn't feel threatened. His life was so completely different from mine, equally exotic and incomprehensible, that it seemed too far away to do any harm. I was a voyeur, an extra. My house was only a hundred yards up the street, but it was miles and miles away.

When I returned home, I stared at Mom's garden, the

finely-trimmed lawn, and the blue sky shimmering in the pool, a reflected world washed clean of consequence. At the dinner table, I ate with visions of Billy's house safely tucked away inside me.

***

Since Billy was younger, we never saw each other in school. I was closer in age to Maggie and sometimes I'd see her at the bus stop or in the corner of the library. If the hallway was empty, sometimes we'd wave to each other, our hands never any higher than our hips. Most of the time, we looked the other way.

My mother and I often saw Billy's mom walking around town in her bathrobe. She limped up a quiet side street, her face caged in black hair. She shuffled along the white line, cars whipping by at forty miles an hour, her bathrobe undulating in heavy waves like a waterlogged cape.

"That poor woman," my mother said, her tongue clicking on the back of her teeth.

We never stopped to give her a ride. We thought about her only when we saw her and drove on.

I didn't want to associate with Billy or his family outside of his house. Inside his house, I was not myself. I was Billy's protégé, his understudy in the ways of evil, learning how to be bad. Outside, I was the polite, chubby, red-cheeked child with the permanent smile who always got along with others. I was known for my ability to share. But inside, I longed to learn Billy's language, to communicate with the world the way he did.

It was the opposite for Billy. Outside of his house, he

felt vulnerable and weak. Once, I invited him to visit my grandparents in New Jersey. He agreed, and I imagine I felt comfortable with the situation because we'd be far away from our hometown and no one would know us. My parents asked me if I wouldn't rather take another friend, someone I knew better. They didn't know as well as I did what went on in Billy's house, but they sensed something, as if a sinister soundtrack became audible as soon as Billy appeared. As my father loaded Billy's backpack into the car, he looked at me as if I might still change my mind.

Billy didn't talk the entire trip. Not one word. Nor did I see him eat anything. When my grandmother asked him if he'd like some lasagna or a slice of meatloaf, he just shook his head and sat at the table with his head down. Though he was obviously uncomfortable, I marveled at the power he had over the table, each of us not sure how to behave in his presence.

***

Josephina was five, but still couldn't talk. She communicated in one-syllable sounds and hand gestures. She'd point to a box of chicken McNuggets and open her mouth wide, waiting for someone to feed her. She'd squeal and scream, reaching for a can of soda on the counter until someone boosted her up. When she wanted to go outside, she scratched at the door like a small dog begging to escape.

With her bucket of multi-colored chalk, she drew bright worlds on the hot black driveway. Smiling yellow suns coaxed laughing purple flowers from tall magenta grass. Herds of unicorns and giraffes and dinosaurs ran together through open fields. She sang songs to herself in her own language, baby talk much too young for her, as if there were an infant ventriloquist hiding behind her, controlling every word she said and lyric she sang.

Billy rode his bike up and down the driveway, screeching to a stop over her drawings until her worlds were blurry and his bike tires were coated with chalk. His mother and sister yelled and chased him down the driveway as he peddled just enough to stay ahead of them, laughing. I sat in the grass, the urge to stop him surging up in me, to kick Billy from his bicycle with the tip of my sneaker like a peasant suddenly spearing the dragon with his sword. But I didn't. I watched Josephina stand above her world crying, a stub of chalk in her hand, wondering where to start.

***

One day, Billy and I were in Maggie's room. Maggie was downstairs. Their mother was asleep. Josephina sat on the edge of Maggie's bed as we flipped through a dirty magazine and dialed the numbers in the back. We used Maggie's telephone, the trendy kind made of clear plastic so all of the inner workings were visible. The transparent receiver blinked in Billy's hand.

"What's that?" he said. "You want to speak to Anthony? Okay. Here he is."

Billy tried handing me the phone but I ran to the other side of the room, tripping over Josephina's Twister mat. He laughed and gave the phone to Josephina instead. I picked up the cordless phone on the table and listened. A woman on the other end moaned softly, asking Josephina what she wanted. She said she wanted to please Josephina and make all her fantasies come true. *You'd like that, wouldn't you, baby?* Josephina seemed soothed by the voice, as if listening to a nursery rhyme. Billy hung up the phone and Josephina screamed, holding the phone to her ear, slapping all the buttons, trying to make the voice come back.

This is when I would leave. Josephina would scream and Billy's mom would wake up and run to her—*What? What is it? What's the matter?*—but Josephina couldn't tell her, couldn't speak her language. She'd just scream and reach out in the air for some invisible savior. I'd slip out the back door and run home.

I slept over there only once. In the middle of the night, I began to sleepwalk. I got up from my bed and walked down the stairs. Somehow, I made it through the obstacle course of toys and dishes on the living room floor and into the kitchen. My hands searched the walls for the door knob and as I began to turn it, Billy's mother touched my shoulder.

"Anthony," she whispered, "where are you going?"

Her question woke me, and I was suddenly inches from her face, her wrinkled olive skin, long thin black hair. She looked like a zombie. She was breathing heavy; she must have chased me.

"Home," I said. "I have to go home."

"It's late, though. You can go home in the morning." She turned me around and sent me back through the house, back upstairs, back to Billy's room.

In the middle of the night, I heard Billy guiding Josephina down the dark hallway, into his room. The rustling of Billy's blanket. Josephina's mysterious language. Billy whispered; she giggled. Silence. Then I heard only Billy, no words, only breath.

In the morning, Josephina was gone. Billy was sleeping. I snuck out the back door and walked home, no one there to stop me.

***

Though I couldn't see in the darkness, Billy and Josephina's sounds drew pictures in my mind like chalk on asphalt. I felt I could no longer safely watch lest I be responsible for what I was witnessing.

But I continued to go over there. It was not my life.

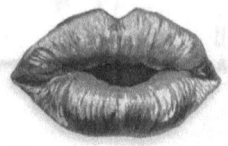

Getting Busted in a Porn Emporium

By David Henry Sterry

This is not a story about losing my innocence. This is a story about stealing someone else's. One of my hobbies is going into pornographic bookstores where they have booths you can sit in, watch filthy movies, and masturbate, all for a modest fee. So I was in Hollywood, minding my own business. All these stories start like this—that would be the name of the show, if they made a show about my life—the *Minding My Own Business* show. It's a Friday night, a little quiet cuz it's early still, 10:30, and I walk into Porn R Us. I mosey back to a booth. There are no doors on the booths; only curtains. I go into a booth, pull the curtain shut, put a dollar into the slot, and, when the eagle disappears, the movies start. I surf through the collection of high quality adult entertainment until I find one that suits me. I start getting busy with myself. Let's be clear, the curtain was closed, there was nobody else in the whole arcade area, but I did have myself out in hand manually pleasuring myself.

Boom! A guy peeks his head in my booth.

"Naw, thanks, not interested," I say, thinking he was a nice man looking to give me some fellatio.

Wrong!

He is a cocksucker, but a very different kind. He is in fact a member of LA's finest, plainclothed, with a female partner. They are Gap-friendly, non-descript. They handcuff me.

"Is that really necessary?" I ask.

It's just procedure, they explain. Apparently LAPD is very big on procedure when they're not bashing unarmed black men with billy clubs. So they take me to the station and on the way I say, "Is this really why you became a cop? To arrest guys whacking off in porn stores? Is this what you dreamed the job would be? I mean it's a porno store for God's sake, that's what it's made for—I wasn't bothering anybody, the curtain was closed, the only person I was abusing was me. This is a perfect metaphor for everything that's wrong with America. The masturbator who pays his taxes and who minds his own business and who's just having some good clean fun gets busted while the rapists and the nasty pimps and the billionaire stock frauder's who lose family's fortunes walk around free as a jay bird."

They laugh, I'll give 'em that. They say that just between them and me they hated getting the porn assignment, they argued against it, it's just an easy way for the city to make money, they are on a quota, as soon as they catch their limit they get to go back to vice.

Feels good to bond. Gives me hope for America, that the criminal masturbator and the LA cop can find common ground and commiserate about what's wrong with our great country. They book me. Smile nicely.

I am chained to a bench next to a kid. He asks me what I'm in for.

"I killed a couple of guys, but they had it comin'."

The kid backs away as far as his chain will let him.

"Killing changes a man." I say in my low scary voice. "I recommend it for everyone. Especially if you do it with your bare hands."

I really enjoy going from criminal masturbator to bare-handed killer.

They take my fingerprints and my picture. The guy makes me have my picture taken three times. He keeps saying I look too happy. I can't help it, I explained, I'm an actor, I like having my picture taken.

I am released within twenty minutes. They reduce the charge to misdemeanor masturbator with intent to ejaculate or something. A slap on the wanking wrist. Cost me like a hundred bucks.

But the look of terror and respect on the kid's face as I stole his innocence when he found out I was a mad crazy killer made the whole thing worth it.

Bad Medicine

By Tiffanie Gabrielse

My high school, until my fourteenth year, was a building of beauty. Three floors of inspiring orange railings (our school colors) and large windows made for an equally massive and impressive atrium entry way. The sun always shined and, when my friends gathered around me in the morning, so did I.

Once a week at three o'clock, my life grew bigger, brighter, balanced—equal. Despite my rare form of dwarfism, I felt pride when I waddled down the corridors and through a particular set of heavy fire doors. I was always accompanied by my best friend, Megan, and together we traveled toward the sports medicine room. I was a budding individualist, marching toward a clan of students who aimed to learn about the one subject I already knew all too well: medicine. My entire life had been one surgery after another. In fact, it was all I knew. And I couldn't wait to wear my team jacket—after getting the length of the arms taken in, of course.

The cabinet of trophies and school pride sparkled, twinkled

and glowed under the lights. I wanted to do my part for the school that I believed in; for the school that I thought believed in me. I wanted to help add more championship medals to our impressive collection. I could, and I would, I thought, by joining the sports medicine team, by caring for those on the field. If anyone understood injury, physical pain and the importance of compassion, it was me.

Despite being with the team for only three weeks, I had lofty expectations and ideals. I wanted more than anything to motivate my team. I would be their rock, their inspiration, their happy face.

It was a small room but I was small too—we fit. I believed it was meant to be. Each time we gathered together our sports medicine coach, Ms. H., would be the last to enter the room. She never smiled or returned the gesture, she never exuded happiness. Everything was just business. It never struck me as personal or odd. Ignorantly, I ventured it to just be her way.

Everyday her hair ran the same wild path down her back. She was tall, a woman with pale skin and small, icy eyes. Unfortunately, I hadn't yet discovered that her most salient characteristics were her ignorance and her insensitivity.

To the right of the room, stacks of shelves rested against the wall; to the left were blue, padded tables on which the athletes could lay; in the back, tucked into a corner, stood an ice machine. On this particular day our training exercise was about empathizing with the athletes.

"We're going to fill this trash bucket with ice," Ms. H. said plainly, as she scooped ice out of the machine, poured it into the cylindrical container and let the lid slam shut. "When you're on the field and there's an injury, we apply ice. Sometimes the ice feels worse than the injury, but our job is to make sure they keep it on their bodies. How can we tell them to do this if, we don't know what the cold feels like? For five minutes you are all going to take turns placing your foot in this bucket." She plopped the bucket beside one of the blue padded tables.

My rare form of dwarfism plays on the same team as extreme arthritis and cold has always been a great conductor of pain. I knew, without actually understanding the logistics of it at the time, my bones, my muscles and my body as a whole would react horribly. I shuddered inside, knowing that my pain would continue long past the five minutes and thinking about the inevitable sleepless and uncomfortable night waiting for me should I follow through with this exercise.

I could have been flippant, I could have made an excuse to leave (I initially wanted to) or I could have been a smart ass. *Obviously, it's going to be cold. It's ice. Obviously, the athletes will feel discomfort. It's a fresh injury pressed against frozen, rough cubes. Duh.* But I didn't do any of that. I wanted to belong. I wanted to be liked. I wanted to be normal.

I decided to trust my coach—my leader—with the truth.

"Ms. H.," I squeaked. "Can I talk to you for a second?"

She stomped toward me and hovered like a disdainful god.

"Can I tell you something? Over here?" I moved to an empty corner of the room across from the ice machine.

She was reluctant to move away from the students already taking off their shoes and socks. Eventually, she met me in the corner, her expression hard.

I tried to speak softly. I didn't want to disturb everyone with my extended history of hospital visits. "I've had a lot of surgery on my feet," at that point, my voice cracked, I never had to explain my body before, "and if I take off my shoes and socks and place my foot in the ice, I think it's going to hurt worse than it should. I don't think it's a good idea. Would it be alright if I put my hand in the ice instead? I'll still feel the cold and I'll still understand the athletes. I haven't had surgery on my hands. See?" I held up my hand and smiled.

For what seemed like an eternity I waited for a reaction. Finally, she exhaled and walked away. Beneath the shelves towering against the wall, she reached for something. In one swift crude movement, she brought two egg crates to the center of the room. Their edges slapped the floor.

"Let's talk." Her tone matched the chilled air. With her hand she motioned for me to leave the corner, sit on a crate, and face her.

Everyone pretended to be too busy to notice. But they weren't too busy. They knew, by the manner in which she was waiting for me to enter the center of the room, that though the ice had melted, her heart would never thaw.

They knew, because they were subjected to a form of it at some point before, that with every step closer I was about to enter into an ugly adulthood. I was about to be punished for challenging her tyranny. Who did I think I was?

Ms. H. inhaled deeply, opened her mouth, and took aim for my soul. "I don't know what kind of disease you have but, *obviously*, you're a dwarf. Why don't you tell me what you can and cannot do?"

Her words flung into the air, dropped to the floor and shattered into a million pointed pieces around me. The jagged edges of each letter embedded deep into my skin.

I said nothing.

No one did anything to help, to stop the attack.

Unsatisfied and determined to beat me until every breath I had left was gone, determined to drive those sharp pieces further, she struck me again: "Maybe this isn't the right activity for you. I know you agree, don't you?"

Each word sliced and burned.

Do I have a disease? Is there something wrong with the way I am? Why haven't my parents ever told me something was wrong with me? Why haven't my friends?

I felt alone. Why had everyone lied to me? I was raised to believe that I was just like everyone else, that my only enemy was fear. Lies—all lies!

Emotions I had never experienced flooded my core: anger, hostility, aggression, rage, hate. I discovered it all.

Her words never existed in the world my parents and friends built for me, but that day, she destroyed all their hard work with a sentence. Nothing would be the same, including me. The light within me dimmed. Despite the feelings fighting to enslave my innocence within, I remained quiescent. I forced myself to be acceptant of her narrow mind.

Maybe I deserved it.

In the distance, I heard something shatter: It was my confidence. My blood sizzled as it coursed around and around in my veins. My heart raced outrageously. I could feel it trying to fly out of my chest. I wanted to escape and explode. Eyes wide, and for the first time open, I had no choice but to allow the assault.

Who was I to fight back? Was I allowed to fight? How does one fight? I was only fourteen.

Quietly, I stood up. She stood as well, gathered the egg crates and slid them back to their original location. No one said a word; the only sound was the ticking wall clock as it timed my exit.

I gathered my things and noticed that my peers kept up their awkward act. Some fiddled with medical tape. Some deconstructed and then restacked rolls of wrapped bandages. No one looked at me. They didn't know what to do. Maybe, if they pretended not to hear it, then it wasn't happening.

Then, for the first time, she smiled at me. As I headed to the door she finally split her thin lips and extended a grin across her smug face. She acted as if she had saved the team from future hardship, as if she genuinely hated to be the bearer of bad news, as if she had a soul and meant no harm in torching the veil over my eyes. It had to burn at some point. Someone had to do it eventually.

I stepped quickly out to the hall and journeyed the corridor—alone. The memorabilia along the wall were now tarnished trinkets. The heavy fire doors that I once believed could open into a life of acceptance, of being a part of something, a team, now morphed into an ominous and cynical creature. Double metal handles formed a bent nose. Slender, vertical upper windows were a set of unforgiving eyes. The sliver of light down the center, lips.

Would I be able to break through? To return to the world I once knew?

I remember how small my hands looked pressed flat against the faux wood. How pathetic and disjointed. I struggled to push beyond them. The air suddenly went thick and sour. It smelled of a stench I can now name: high school, and the world encircling it, darkening to black. The vibrant orange railing lost its color. The shiny floor lost its luster. The world lost its beautiful clarity and, instead, was replaced with blurry acres of congested weeds and muddy waters. This teacher revealed the truth: The world is ugly. She revealed that I was not as courageous as I believed. Her words told me that I was different, strange, an outcast, that just because I wanted to do something, didn't mean that I could. Just as much as any surgery, her words scarred me. Even though it was painful, the damage her words inflicted taught me a valuable lesson: Words have power. That was a power that I could wield—no matter my size.

Excerpt from Some Girls: My Life in a Harem

By Jillian Lauren

Day tumbled into night tumbled into party time. I could barely change my shoes fast enough to keep up. When we dressed for the party, I chose my best suit because it was sexy and was actually the most expensive item of clothing I owned. I hoped it might inspire some confidence.

Destiny, Serena, and I waited for Ari in the foyer. As I grew accustomed to it, the house was looking less like a palace and more like a banquet hall. I pictured a gaggle of bridesmaids posed on the staircase. But it was just the three of us, facing each other awkwardly, tallying up each other's flaws and assets as we waited for Ari's entrance. I figured that over Destiny and her acrylic claws, I had looks but not wildness. Over Serena and her china-doll eyes, I had smarts but not looks.

Serena leaned against a column opposite me. She was the blonde and I was the brunette. In the world of musical theater, she would be the soprano and I the alto. I was the one with the big ass who played her lines for laughs. Serena was the slender-waisted ingénue who got the guy in the end. I was Rizzo and she was Sandy. I was Ado Annie and she was what's-her-name in the surrey. We faced off until, with a subtle shift in posture, she dismissed me as not much of a threat. One thing Sandy always forgets is that Rizzo has the best song in the show.

The palace was too far to walk, so we drove the golf carts that were parked in our carport. Ari drove with Destiny and I hopped on with Serena, who silently steered through the winding, lit pathways, past the pools and tennis courts and palm trees. The air was humid and thick with the fragrance of tropical flowers. Not an hour out of the shower, I already felt sticky. My head raced with plans. I would make the best of my time here. I would improve my tennis game. I would get a tan. I would lose weight. And maybe I would even make a prince fall in love with me and my whole life would change in dazzling and unexpected ways. I longed for a magic pill to soothe the restlessness that prickled constantly under my skin. I'm not sure what made me think I'd find it in Brunei, but I wouldn't be the first person who hoped to step off a plane on the other side of the world and discover their true self standing there waiting for them.

Up close the palace reminded me of a picture I had seen once of Hearst Castle, on the California Coast. There were gold domes, columns, and twin marble staircases that curved like ribbons up to the main entrance.

"We normally go in the side because it's less of a hike, but I want you guys to see the entrance hall," said Ari. "I think you'll like it."

We were breathing hard when we reached the top of the stairs. We entered a cavernous cathedral of a room with a fountain at the center. I felt like I had walked onto the set of some 1930s MGM movie version of *Salome*. Surely a flock of harem-pants-clad showgirls was about to descend the stairs and launch into a Busby Berkeley dance number.

"It's all real," said Serena.

"Real what?"

"Like, the gold in the carpet is real gold. That ruby is a real ruby," she said, pointing at a ceramic tiger that stood near the fountain. The tiger held in its mouth a round, red stone the size of a tennis ball.

I spotted what looked like a Picasso directly across from the front door—also real, I assumed. We followed Ari around a corner and there, where a hallway bisected the main foyer, a Degas ballerina sculpture stood on a pedestal, a little girl cast in bronze. She clasped her arms behind her back and pushed her chest out defiantly, her foot thrust in front of her in third position. It looked exactly like the one that I had loved visiting as a child, when my father would take me to the Metropolitan Museum of Art on special Sundays to wander the wondrous galleries and then stuff ourselves with hot dogs on the steps. Each visit we chose a different gallery. We sat on a bench in front of a giant Jackson Pollock and looked for charging bulls and blooming irises and skywriters hiding in the paint splatter. We crossed our eyes and tried to reassemble the figures cut to pieces by Picasso. We stood washed in light next to the enormous wall of windows that faces the Temple of Dendur and told stories of time travel. But at the end of the day we always visited my Degas ballerinas, numinous and frozen in time, pinned like butterflies to the wall.

When she caught me staring at the sculpture, Ari told me that Robin was an avid art collector. He had countless walls to decorate. Robin owned other palaces where he lived, still others where his three wives lived, whole office buildings where he conducted business, and hotels and estates in Singapore, London, and Los Angeles. But Ari informed me that some of his favorite art was right here. We were standing in the palace where he unwound every night, his sunny pleasure dome.

"Come on," she said, with a hint of trepidation. "Let's go in."

We were so close I could have walked up and touched the Degas. In fact, I felt an overwhelming compulsion to do just that. I made a note to try to sneak back and do it sometime later. Like people touch the feet of Jesus on the Pietà and hope for a blessing, I would touch the feet of the dancer and hope for grace.

Prom Queen

By Valley Haggard

After driving past a dozen stands on the side of the road selling vegetables, we pass a green highway sign that says, "Gateway, Arkansas; Population: 67."

"This is it," says Will Jr. "But I'll have to change that sign." He laughs. "Sixty-seven plus us. *Sixty-nine.*"

Going to live with his recently widowed dad in Arkansas seems like a better option than waiting tables in Virginia and living with my mom. On the road, we take turns driving and camping in my little tent with only half its poles. The heat he generates in the sleeping bag is almost enough to make me love him.

Last summer Will Jr. asked me to marry him on a dude ranch in Colorado. He'd been a wrangler and I'd been a cabin girl, but after getting pregnant, I'd given him his ring back. I was twenty-two and not ready to be anyone's mother, or wife.

Arkansas, however, with its shaggy fields of bulls and

buffalos stretched between doublewides and junk stores, I love instantly. In a new place like this, anything can happen. I pray that it will. Will Jr. tells me that his relationship with his old man isn't easy and I ask him to tell me any relationships that are. "Us," he says, "you and me." But I begin to count cows instead of answering him and he jiggles his knee up and down for the rest of the drive, turning at last on to a dirt road which winds through the trees to his father's farm. Will Sr. is waiting for us on the front porch of a wood cabin, a cigarette dangling between his lips as if he's been there all day. He is wearing a red flannel shirt, a white t-shirt, blue jeans, leather boots and a cowboy hat. He's not exactly handsome, but his blue eyes light up bright when he sees us and the white hair swirling around his temples seems a wild sort of distinguished.

"Welcome to your new home," he says, leading us through the overgrown field to the blockhouse, a small metal shack about a hundred yards past his cabin. A bare double mattress is crammed between raw lumber and a tangle of shovels and rakes. Will Jr. pushes our canvas army sack through the cobwebs under a workbench. I sit down on the mattress and watch dust float up around my thighs. There is no sink or toilet and I can't name half of the rusted tools or machines on the shelves above our heads, but at least this is completely different from what I've left behind.

"We'll take it," I say. "Home, sweet home."

Before we unpack, the three of us squeeze into the front of Will Sr.'s Dodge pickup and cross the county line to Ruby's Liquor Store. Will Sr. talks to Ruby about his chickens and asks if she knows anyone selling buffalo hides. Will Jr. and

I have $27 left between us and we spend it on a carton of cigarettes, a bottle of whiskey and a pound of bacon for the morning.

When we return, we listen to country music and shuck red and orange kernels of Indian corn. I prefer liquor, but Will Sr. insists on making us Blackberry Cadillacs, Manischewitz wine splashed with ginger ale. The biting sweetness makes my head heavy and empty at the same time. Then it becomes the feeling I most like, of being intimately familiar with something still brand new. I know that Will Sr. built this cabin by hand and I admire the intricate animal faces he has carved into walking sticks in a bucket by the door, but I also notice the dust and cobwebs that have accumulated in the cracks of everything. He is still grieving, I think. This place could use a woman's touch.

A baby horse is born before dawn the next morning. Will Jr. and I are drinking coffee on the front porch when Will Sr. carries her up from the meadow, cradling her like a human infant instead of fifty pounds of still trembling horseflesh. I sense that even though he hasn't always lived alone, he is more comfortable with horses than people.

He grunts as he sets the baby down in front of her mother, a black mare named Lacy. Only hours old, the baby is all awkward grace, legs akimbo, solid red with a white stripe stretching from her ears to the tip of her nose. She teeters for a moment on her long, spindly legs before collapsing into the straw. Lacy nudges her with her massive head and then turns away and begins to munch on hay from her trough. Her teats drip milk into the dirt instead of into her baby's mouth.

I watch as the foal tries to stand up and then prances and stumbles like a teenager who can't figure out where to put her feet. Will Sr. brings her to Lacy's nipple again and again, but she won't take it so he goes into the house to create a mixture he'll spend the next month perfecting: molasses and formula, vitamins, iron and oats. He slices the nipple on the bottle in half for a faster suck then hands it to me. I glide it into her mouth. So this is what it would have been like to feed a baby, I think. "I'm going to name her Morning Feather," Will Sr. says. "Do you like that, Cowgirl?"

I nod that I do, but because she is so beautiful and so completely out of control, I call her Prom Queen instead.

We've been on the farm for less than a week when Will Jr. slams a hammer into the back of his hand, leaving an angry red dent. "I was making a bench for you to sit on while you fed her," he explains, pointing to Prom Queen.

"Thanks," I say, "but you shouldn't have." At 6'4" he is bigger than a horse, and clumsier. I don't say it, but I know he still keeps the wedding ring I returned to him in the pocket of his jeans.

"It'd be better if you had made it with intersecting joints," says Will Sr., who has come in with oats for the horses.

"You make it then," says Will Jr., tossing the half finished bench to his dad.

"OK," says Will Sr., snagging the bench out of the air. "Let me have her."

Will Sr. is careful and patient with me and doesn't mind answering all of my questions, but when Will Jr. drags the lawnmower over a cluster of arm-sized roots, it's another story.

"You're just like King Midas, son," Will Sr. says, inspecting the damage to the blade. "But everything you touch turns to shit."

When I'm not nursing the baby, Will Sr. teaches me how to repair fence line, haul hay and harvest the vegetables in the garden. He shows me where to cut the plants—at the root or the stalk—and I pay attention because it means the difference between a box of macaroni or a big salad of comfrey and mustard greens. He gives me his wife's acrylics and as we walk the property line, I take careful notes about the flowers so I can paint them later. *The purple flowers outside the blockhouse are Luminaria. Lilacs line the far fence. Next to the walking sticks are Columbine. Narcissus is white, near the well.*

We hand-roll Turkish tobacco and smoke the pot Will Sr. grows in the far field. We drink whiskey and Blackberry Cadillacs. One day we saddle up Lacy and the mule for a ride into the woods. I get scratches on my arms from the brambles but they are the kind of scars I'm proud of. I hope they will last. Instead of coming with us, Will Jr. flies his yellow dragon kite above the tree line. That night when he rolls toward me in our bed, I pretend that I'm asleep.

When I hold a chicken just hatched from its egg or make tea from freshly picked chamomile, I feel as if I could live on this farm forever. I think of my dad, who I'd always wanted to marry, but who had instead married everyone else, including at one point, my mother. I like Will Sr.'s stories, but I miss my dad's jokes, his broad shoulders and deep brown eyes, his cheek bones, higher than an Indian Chief's. It's funny, I think, now that my dad finally has his own farm and his final wife, I'm the one on the move with a temporary address.

When my mother calls I tell her how happy I am here with the Wills, living the life of a farmer. "Oh Valley," she says. "How will you ever learn to live with just one man?"

When they tell me they are going to slaughter a goose for our supper, I decide to watch. I have never seen anything killed before, but I know that living on a farm requires certain sacrifices. Will Jr. grips the belly while his father steadies the neck. The goose does not go easily and Will Sr. has to use his axe like a saw to get from one end of the neck to the other. I don't allow myself to blink until the last jagged blow when Will Sr. slices through his own thumb. A stubby piece of flesh dangles from a thin flap of skin and I follow him into the kitchen where he sets the goose's feet on the counter. I hold my breath, dumping cayenne pepper into his open vein as he instructs, watching his blood pump into the sink, mingling with the goose's before swirling down the drain. That night we eat goose breast for dinner, storing the legs in the freezer, wrapped in foil.

"Cowgirl," says Will Sr. "I need your help." He leads me into his bedroom and opens the closet, where all of his wife's clothes still hang as if she might come back and wear them again. "They've all got to go and I can't do it," he says. I am happy that he needs me so I gather garbage bags from the kitchen and begin to take stock of the pinks, blues and yellows, the cottons, wools and polyesters.

But instead of bagging them up, I try them on. Between the king size bed and the full-length mirror, I slip on blouses, wranglers and pink silk lingerie. I make a tidy stack on the bed of what fits, stuffing into the bag what doesn't. Last, on a shelf in the back of the closet, I find her wedding dress. It is pressed and perfect, preserved in its dry cleaner's bag like a gift. I tug it on over my head and smile when the white lace hugs my curves in all the right places. I stare at myself in the mirror; the apparition of a bride stares back. I think about our two bodies, hers in the ground and mine emptier than it's ever been. This is what I would have looked like, I think, if I had married Will Jr. I hope to God that I've made the right decision.

As Prom Queen gets worse instead of better, I offer to sleep with her in the barn. Will Sr. has put an IV into her thigh and Lacy has been trying to bite it out. It has been raining for days and the barn is damp but I feel like someone must keep an eye on the baby. "You sure are a good sport," Will Sr. says.

"Well, Jesus slept in a barn," I say, but I don't feel at all like Jesus. The first abortion I'd had in Denver didn't take, so I'd gone back and made them do it again.

Every time we hear the high-pitched howl of a coyote, Lacy bucks wildly but Prom Queen lies glassy-eyed on the matted hay. I massage her back, wrapping her in a blanket and feeding her Lacy's milk from the cup of my hands. After a while, she walks around in halting circles on her long spindly legs, like she's the lead in a complicated dance number, one where only she hears the music. I finally curl up in the hay, trying to think of a lullaby I can sing that will put us both to sleep.

Will Sr. wakes me up in the morning with a cup of strong, hot coffee. "I want you to have Morning Feather, Cowgirl," he says. "I'm giving her to you." She is the biggest gift I've ever received, and by far the most terrible.

That afternoon in the blockhouse, Will Jr. pulls a needle and thread through a rip in his yellow kite. "My sister called," he says. "I'm going to California to visit her. She's sick." I feel my stomach rise and drop.

"When are you leaving?" I ask, taking a long drag from my cigarette.

In the morning we pile into the Dodge and drive to the bus depot two towns over. I'm surprised at the sadness that fills my throat when Will Jr. lifts me two feet off the ground in a crushing hug. "I'll be back in a few weeks," he says. "Wait for me."

"Bye son," says his dad and they pound each other on the back, more like two wild animals than father and son. Will Jr. waves to me from his seat on the bus, his body filling up the entire window. I blow him a kiss and climb into the cab of Will Sr.'s truck. I am completely alone with him for the first time since arriving in Arkansas.

We drive back to the farm in silence.

"I'm going to fix us a drink, Cowgirl," says Will Sr., pulling up in front of the cabin. "I'll be right back," I say and walk to the barn to check on the baby. Her red ears are still soft, but her eyes are the shiny glass of a broken ornament. I sit with her, stroking the fur between her bony shoulders. "She's gone," I tell Will when I come in, and he takes one of my hands and holds it between the two of his.

We finish our drinks and then fix a thermos of whiskey to take with us to the blockhouse where we each pick out a shovel from above the bed. The sky is tinted an eerie shade of indigo and sweat trickles down the small of my back as we dig a grave beneath the cherry tree, deep and narrow enough for a queen. I cradle Prom Queen's shoulders and he steadies her legs as we lower her into her grave.

That night I sleep with Will Sr. in his king sized bed. I hope that he can do the same things to me that he's done to the animal heads he's carved out of wood, making something out of nothing. I don't think about whether it's right or wrong only that it's easier to forget about a baby beneath the weight of a man.

In the morning, I wake up screaming. I have been buried alive—clear snakes and hairy spiders crawl all over my exposed skin, in my ears and out from the hollow of my throat. Will Sr. kisses me on the mouth until I stop shaking.

"Breathe, Cowgirl," he says, leading me to a bouquet of red clover and comfrey he has arranged on the dining room table. And I do breathe, gulping down huge breaths of fresh morning air.

At noon I set a ladder against the cherry tree, across from the grave, on firm ground. I spend hours collecting shiny crimson beads in a bright yellow bucket and then hours more pitting them until my fingers are stained burgundy with juice. This is the first pie I've made from scratch and I concentrate on the way the sugar mixes with the cherry meat, thick and juicy red. In the afternoon, we make thirteen jars of cherry jam—a devil's dozen—boiling the pectin and the cherries, adding mango and orange peel, ladling the thick, sweet syrup into jars. We drink cans of beer while we wait for the lids to pop. I draw horses lying beneath cherry trees on labels that read "My Bitter-Sweet Summer Cherry Jam." At the end of the day we eat huge slabs of pie. Sated at last, Will Sr. presents me with a pair of ruby earrings that once belonged to his wife.

The phone rings the next morning while I'm frying the last of the goose and Will Sr. is picking seeds out of a fresh batch of marijuana. It is Will Jr. who has arrived safely in California and wants to know if I'll meet him in Colorado. He'd rather not return to Arkansas and I don't blame him. I tell him yes and then no and then maybe and when I hang up, I throw myself into Will Sr.'s arms. "He thinks I'm an angel that can do no wrong," I sob into his shoulder.

"That makes two of us, Cowgirl," he says, separating my hair, strand by strand from the smears of wet rolling down my cheek. I allow him to comfort me, but I wonder who I am—the woman that owns my body, or the girl inside of my head, who is both trying to take the world apart and put it back together.

White Lie

By Corey Ginsberg

"Instead of counting by eights, let's spend the rest of class talking about a field trip we'll be going on next week—on the last day of school," Mrs. Pershun said to my second grade class. The words came out of her mouth slowly as she moved the counting chart back to its corner on the side of the chalkboard. She put a lid on the marker that smelled like blueberries—she'd been using it to show us patterns of numbers—and placed it back into the box that went on the blue bookshelf next to her desk.

Even though it was Friday and the little hand was almost on the three, the room was quiet—the kind of quiet it only was when we were in trouble or supposed to be reading to ourselves. The strips of sun that were on the floor by Peter's desk in the morning had moved almost the whole way to Steven's desk, and that meant the bell was about to ring and it would be time to line up for our buses.

None of us moved. We looked at Mrs. Pershun, who wiped

sweat off the side of her face with the white handkerchief she carried in the pocket of her shiny brown pants. She always told my class that we were young, and sweating was easier for young people. When you got to be as old as her, she said, sweating was hard. I wondered if that was why she was going to be retiring, from all the hard sweat.

"Who would like to know where we'll be going?" Mrs. Pershun asked while leaning back on Jenny's desk like she sometimes did when her feet hurt and her ankles got swollen. She said that she was allowed to sit on the desk because she was old, but that we had perfectly good chairs that were perfectly good for sitting on.

We all raised our hands at the same time. My class had only gone on one field trip the entire year—to the Aviary to look at birds—and it was the kind of boring that made my feet tired and my head hurt. The stupid birds flew in circles and squeaked like they hated each other. That was all they did. Everyone in my grade stood by the cages and watched them for a really long time, and then we got back onto the bus. The only good part about the field trip was that we got to eat at McDonald's on the way home, and I ordered chicken nuggets and French fries and ice cream.

"We will be going to Florida—to Disney World, to be exact—and it will be your job to plan everything about this trip," Mrs. Pershun said.

At first I thought my ears heard wrong. Did she really say "Disney World?" Was she serious? I wanted to scream that Disney World was my favorite place on the whole planet, and that she better not be kidding.

"The real Disney World?" Jimi asked from his seat in the front row. He didn't raise his hand.

"Yes, the real Disney World. We will be there for one week, which is six nights and seven days."

"But how are we gonna get there?" Timmy shouted. He ran his hand over top of his spiky hair and down the little ponytail on his neck.

"That's the fun part." There was a smile on Mrs. Pershun's lips but her face was trying to pretend it wasn't there. She couldn't fool me, though; I could tell she was excited. Her fingers tapped on the wood and one of her black shoes with the big soles and Velcro straps went back and forth in the air. "How many of you have ever driven a golf cart?"

The whole classroom was suddenly full of shouts and waving arms. It sounded like we all had a story about steering a golf cart while our dads or grandpas were golfing.

"I've even driven a real car," Shawna said. "My daddy let me drive his convertible." I didn't believe Shawna because she liked to lie when it was time to talk about somebody who wasn't her. My mom told me that was because she needed attention since her parents didn't give her any.

Mrs. Pershun stood in front of the room with her pointer finger over her lips. That meant she wouldn't talk until we were quiet. All the girls in my class said *shhhhh* really loudly so the boys would stop asking stupid questions and we could hear more about our trip.

"Now listen carefully," Mrs. Pershun said. "It will be your job to plan *everything* for this journey. This is a *lot* of responsibility. You must each select a partner—"

Desks opened and slammed shut, and people shouted and pointed to their friends on the other side of the room. I turned and stared at Tommy, who nodded his head "yes" as soon as our faces met. Tommy wore thick glasses and button-up shirts, and the tips of his feet went out to the sides when he walked, just like a duck. He wasn't very good at saying words with "t" in them, like "this" and "those." We were best friends, and he even let me help him make up a dance routine for "Walk Like an Egyptian" when he was in the talent show.

"So you are *really* gonna let us drive golf carts all the way to Florida?" Jimi asked. His voice sounded like my mom's did when she wanted to know if I had *really* cleaned my room. "I don't have a license!"

"That's not a problem," Mrs. Pershun said. "You and your partner must stay on the sidewalk while you're driving. You don't need a license to drive on the sidewalk, do you?"

Mrs. Pershun had thought of everything. And she was right; I was allowed to ride my bike on any sidewalk in my neighborhood, even though I wasn't allowed to go in the road.

"But what about money?" Josh asked. "My parents said Disney World is expensive."

"I just spoke with Principal McClymonds. Since you were such a good class this year, he said he will give each group a blank check to cover the costs of the trip."

"For real?" Josh bounced in his seat. "That's awesome!"

Some other people asked questions, like they didn't really believe her, but I knew she was telling the truth. Adults didn't tell lies, especially not teachers. I wasn't really sure what a blank check was, but I knew the principal had lots of money. He wore a gray suit with lighter gray stripes, and drove a red Corvette. If anyone could give us a blank check, he could.

Mrs. Pershun smiled bigger, the kind of smile that made her cheeks scrunch into her eyes. "But understand that this is a lot of work. You and your partner must account for every cost. That means on Monday you will need to come in with a list of all the expenses you will have. Then you must add them together and tell me the amount you wish the check to be made out for. Remember to include food, gas, hotels and tickets to Disney World and Epcot."

My chest felt busy, like there was a Jack-in-the-box inside, one crank away from popping up.

"On the final day of school, you will have to bring all the items you will need for the trip. But there's a catch—they must all fit inside your backpack."

Half of me was listening to Mrs. Pershun, and half was thinking about all the stuff I would need to pack. I had so many toys, and I knew my small pink backpack could only hold a few. Did I want two or three big ones or lots of smaller things to play with? What about candy? Would there be room for Fruit Rollups and Snickers bars, or would my mom make me bring a change of clothes instead? Maybe I'd wear all the clothes on top of each other so I'd have room for my train whistle, all four Teenage Mutant Ninja Turtles and both walkie-talkies.

"Are there any questions?" Mrs. Pershun asked.

I had about a thousand questions, and I made sure my hand was really high in the air. I waved my fingers and rocked in my seat so she'd call on me, but Jimi shouted out again. "Are you sure you're not being kidding?"

I watched Mrs. Pershun's face. The bags of skin that hung from her cheeks like water balloons jiggled a little then settled down.

"I certainly am not *being* kidding," she told Jimi. "Next Friday, as you all know, is my last day teaching. I will be retired after that, and I wanted to do something nice for my favorite class. Did I ever tell you that you're my favorite class?" We all nodded because she'd told us that—lots of times.

I ran home from the bus stop so fast my lungs felt like they were full of fire. I was glad I had on my new summer tennis shoes because they helped me to be a quick runner, even when they were untied and the tongue was stuck on the side of my foot. As soon as I got in the front door, I threw my backpack down. My mom walked into the kitchen holding my baby brother in one arm and my little sister in the other. Max had yellow baby food all over his chin and he smelled like bananas, and Lizzie's curls hung in her eyes. She said "Tee" when she saw me, because that's how she said "Corey."

"Where's our phonebook?" I asked as I tore through the papers and books piled on the shelves.

"Who are you calling?"

"Tommy. It's for our vacation to Disney World."

"What?"

I didn't really feel like talking because I had so much to do, but I thought I should let my mom know what was going on so she wouldn't pester me with a thousand million questions later. I told her all about Mrs. Pershun and the trip, but I talked in my out-of-breath voice because there was a lot to say. Even though there were two babies hanging from her, my mom seemed happy because she kept nodding and she didn't even interrupt—not once. I felt a little bad that she couldn't come with me on the trip, but it was kids only. When she played Bridge with the neighbors, it was adults only. And besides, she was a grownup and could do whatever she wanted. She had her own car, and even if it sounded like she was dragging cans behind her when it went up hills, it was big and fast. Plus she had a black credit card she kept in her purse; all she had to do was put it in the machine, type in a secret number, and money came out in a neat stack. If she really wanted to go to Disney World, she could leave whenever she felt like it and didn't have to wait for a blank check.

"So you're doing your homework all ready? It's only Friday!" My mom giggled as she handed me the phonebook from a high-up shelf. "We'll need to make sure we get you some sunscreen before this big journey."

For the next six days all I did was think about Florida. At night when I was supposed to be sleeping, I stared at the glow-in-the-dark stars on my ceiling and planned which rides we'd go on first. Tommy and I agreed Space Mountain was at the top of the list. We'd have to go on it at least ten times. Then we'd ride Thunder Mountain and The Mad Tea Party. We even figured out what souvenirs we'd buy for our families: I'd get Minnie and Mickey Mouse ears for my brother and sister, shirts and matching caps for my parents, and a Donald Duck keychain for my grandma, because he was her favorite.

That week Tommy called Information and got the number for lots of hotels and motels. His mom said we should research to see which ones were the safest and least expensive, but Tommy and I didn't care about that kind of stuff. We wanted a hotel that had a swimming pool and an arcade—the kind that gave you free popcorn at night and donuts for breakfast. We wanted a place with bouncy beds and HBO and R-rated movies like *Friday the Thirteenth*, one with a glass elevator and an ice machine on every floor. Tommy called tons of hotels and made a list that took up two pages in his big yellow tablet. He wanted to call more—to be sure we had the best one—but his mom said it was too expensive to keep making long distance calls. So we decided the Marriot in Orlando was good enough.

We added the price of the hotel for six nights to the cost of gas, forty-two Happy Meals and fourteen banana splits. The number kept getting bigger and bigger. My dad told us to remember to include tolls, too, so we put them on the list. We thought of everything, even who should drive first. I told Tommy I should because I was two weeks older, but he said he was taller so it was better if he did. I said it didn't matter how tall you were, stupid. He told me not to call him names. I said he could drive the whole time we were in Florida if I could have the first turn. After lots more yelling, Tommy said okay, but that he got to pick the radio station.

Each day the group of toys laid out on my dresser changed. At first there were two Pound Puppies, a Super Soaker gun and six slap bracelets. Then I got rid of the gun and threw in some candy necklaces, a bottle of sunscreen and my pink

Kodak camera with a new roll of film. When I tried to fit them all into my backpack, it bulged like a camel hump on my back. Just when I thought it couldn't get any bigger, my mom made me put a toothbrush into the front pocket. Like I was gonna use it.

On Friday morning I had to comb my hair two times, since my bangs wouldn't stay down. They kept pointing to the sides, like arrows that couldn't make up their mind which way to go. When nothing else worked, my mom took a spray bottle and spritzed water onto my forehead so the hair would stick down like a Band-Aid®.

"I'm gonna miss the bus!" I told her. "Lemme go!" Half my body was on the chair, but my hands were reaching for my backpack. When I finally pulled myself free, I skipped to the kitchen door, over the cat, and onto the porch. Lizzie waved her grubby hands in her highchair. Just when I was about to run down the driveway, my mom called to me. Her body was hanging out the door.

"Come give me a goodbye kiss," she said. Even though I usually didn't give her a kiss in the morning, I ran back up the path and hugged her. She handed me a powdered sugar donut. I gave her a pretend kiss on the cheek—the kind where you touch your lips to the person but don't make a kissing sound—and took the donut.

"Have a good trip. And call me from the first rest stop!"

Everyone in my class was talking in their outside voices, the kind we were only supposed to use in gym and during recess.

I could hear them as I walked down the hall, past the rows of red lockers and the black and white checkered floor, past the kindergarteners putting their backpacks in their cubbies and the sixth graders who were too cool to go to their homerooms and were sitting Indian-style in the hallways. When I walked into the classroom, everyone was sitting on their desks. Mrs. Pershun wasn't there yet, and I was glad because she'd have been the kind of angry she got when lots went wrong and she couldn't decide what to yell about first.

In the corner of the classroom by the Counting Chart, desks were pushed together in groups like bunches of grapes. The popular girls argued about which list was for the most money, and the boys had dumped out all their baseball cards into a pile and were fighting over whose was the best. Rachel, Stephanie and Brandon were the only ones who didn't seem excited; they sat with their heads resting in their hands on the top of their desks like this was just an ordinary day. They weren't allowed to eat cupcakes for birthdays or to sing Christmas Carols in school. My mom said it was because they were Jova Witnesses or something like that. Maybe Jova Witnesses weren't allowed to go to Disney World, either.

Tommy sat apart from the rest of the class at his desk in the middle of the room. Even though almost everyone was wearing T-shirts and shorts, Tommy had on a button-up shirt with neon orange flowers and vines printed on it. I was pretty sure it would look perfect once we got to Florida, since that's how people there probably dressed. He was staring at the yellow notepad that had our list on it. Tommy held the paper up close to his face—so close it almost touched his glasses—

and his lips moved.

I put my backpack next to my desk but didn't open it because I knew that if I got it opened, I'd never be able to shut it. Tommy saw me sitting there and came over with the paper in his hands. It had been his job to add the costs together, and he had the final amount circled at the bottom of the page in a big cloud.

"Look at how much money ours is for!" he said, pointing to the number, which was more than one thousand dollars. My cheeks got hot thinking about all that cash. We would have to hide it well; my mom always made me put money in lots of different places when I went out so if I lost some, there would still be more dollars left, hidden in my socks or in the case with my toothbrush. I wondered how we would get the cash—if it would be ten dollar bills or hundred dollar bills. Either way it made me nervous. I hoped Mrs. Pershun would give us all ones so I wouldn't feel bad if I lost some.

Everyone in the classroom suddenly got quiet. I looked up from my desk and saw Mrs. Pershun's face peeking into the door. She sometimes played that game and spied on us to see if we were being bad when she wasn't watching. Shawna and Jenny got off the top of their desks and slid into their seats, and the boys in the front of the room shoved their baseball cards into a big pile and threw them into a desk.

"Well the big day is finally here," Mrs. Pershun said as she put her black purse into the bottom drawer of her desk. She had on a Mickey Mouse shirt, white pants with a crease down the middle and big sunglasses with gold on the sides. She turned her head while she talked so she could look at everyone over top the lenses. "Can you please pass your homework assignments to the front so that I can look at them?"

It sounded like a paper storm as everyone handed their homework to the person in front of them. I watched Tommy pass ours up.

Mrs. Pershun gathered the papers from the first row and hit the pile off her desk until they lined up at the edges into a neat stack. I liked the way she did that, always making them come together into a perfect bunch. Instead of putting them in her desk drawer like she always did, she licked her finger and started to go through the pages. She looked at each paper quickly, and her eyes went back and forth like a ping pong ball. Every few minutes she laughed a little and made a loud sighing sound like she was letting out a chest full of air.

"You all did very well with this assignment," Mrs. Pershun said when she reached the end of the pile, "very well indeed." She folded her hands so her fingers looked like a pack of sausages, then stared at us with the same look my mom had when I caught her sneaking cigarettes in the back yard at night with Mrs. Beswick, the lady who lived down the street.

"Now, can anyone tell me what they learned from this assignment?"

I was confused. What I had learned? Sometimes Mrs. Pershun asked hard questions and she had to say them a different way for us to understand. Maybe this was one of those questions. A few chairs squeaked in the classroom, but other than that, we were the bad kind of quiet that means we don't understand.

"Does nobody know the answer to this question?"

"Math?" someone said in a little voice without raising their hand.

"Good, that's correct. You learned to add up large numbers without the help of the Counting Chart. What else?"

The classroom was silent.

"Well, for one thing, you learned how much planning goes into a trip like this. Now you'll have a new appreciation for your parents! Someday, if you ever *really* get to go to Florida, you will know how expensive it is and how much effort it takes to coordinate a vacation."

There was something about the way Mrs. Pershun said "really" that made me feel hot, cold and sick—all at the same time. The inside of me felt like ketchup and mustard look when I mix them on my plate—the dirty color they turn right after the yellow and red have been swirled too much. Even though the classroom was silent, the sound changed into the kind of quiet that means something's wrong.

Mrs. Pershun looked happy, sitting there on the edge of the desk smiling. She reminded me of my friend Steven's python right after it ate a mouse—like it was so strong it didn't even care about what it had just done. The classroom was full of whimpers and grunts, and Shirley looked like she was going to cry. Tommy stared up at the ceiling, then at the floor beneath his desk. His eyes went all over the place.

Finally, Jimi spoke up. "So you were lying then? We're not really going to Disney World."

"Well, Jimi, it wasn't quite a lie. No, I would call it a 'little fib' or a 'white lie'."

"What's the difference?" he asked. His voice didn't sound

like it really wanted to know the answer.

"A white lie is told to help someone learn something, whereas a *real* lie is done to hurt them."

"But how does lying about getting to go on vacation help us?"

Mrs. Pershun leaned back on the desk and looked at the ceiling. Maybe she didn't notice how angry we were. Or maybe she didn't care. I tried to burn a hole through her with my eyes, like holding a magnifying glass over a leaf on a sunny day, while I said every bad word I could think of in my head—even the really bad ones.

"It was meant as a learning exercise," she said, "to teach you something."

I was all over confused. Why was it okay for Mrs. Pershun to lie to us, but if I ever told a fib—even a small one—I'd be grounded and have to go to detention? I never even realized a teacher could lie. Sure, I knew some adults did, but those were the bad ones in jails, the ones on TV shows late at night that I wasn't allowed to watch. Not teachers. Teachers were supposed to be honest all the time; it was part of their job. If Mrs. Pershun had lied about Disney World, how could I trust anything she'd said all year? What if cursive writing wasn't a real thing? What if it was a language she made up and forced us to practice until our fingers hurt? And the Counting Chart on the front wall—the one she scribbled all over every day as we counted to one hundred by multiples of five, ten and twenty—what if math was really something else?

"One day you'll thank me for this," Mrs. Pershun finally said. Her words meant that she knew everything because she was old and wise, but we had no idea how things worked in the real world because we were stupid seven years olds.

All morning I sat there with my hands on my lap, trying to tune out everything Mrs. Pershun said. It took forever for the little hand to reach the twelve.

Instead of buying pizza for lunch that day, I used my money to get ice cream and fruit punch. I wasn't even that hungry, but I ate the Choco Taco and Scooter Crunch so fast I got a headache between my eyes and above my ears. As soon as I threw away the wrappers, I ran outside onto the field for recess. I played kickball with the boys and imagined the red rubber ball was Mrs. Pershun's ugly fat head. Each time my foot smacked it her face jumped past the infield and fell down near the fence at the edge of the lot.

In the hours after recess, my class was supposed to study spelling, math and social studies. Since it was the last day of school, Mrs. Pershun said we could sit on our desks and talk to each other, or spread out in the room and play board games until the final bell rang. She had the tired face on, and that meant she didn't want to be in charge of talking.

I sat on the floor in the corner with Jimi. We played Chutes and Ladders, and I kept getting the big chute right at the end, which meant I had to go all the way back down to the bottom of the board. Stupid game—just when I got a big ladder, Mrs. Pershun asked us to all come to the front of the room.

Maybe because she felt bad about her white lie or maybe because it was the last day she'd ever have to teach, Mrs. Pershun said we could each choose a special item from her bag of treats. We all moved around the small blue picnic table in the back of the room and watched her dump everything out from her sack. There was a pile of chocolate bars, potato chip bags, cans of Pepsi, and even the counting chart.

"Who would want the counting chart when they could have candy?" Jenny asked in an *eww gross* voice. She grabbed the last Snickers bar and walked back to her game of Old Maid.

The chocolate looked good, and there were even Twix bars—my favorite. But I had an idea that was better than chocolate. I waited till everyone else took the candy and potato chips from the table, then I moved near the counting chart.

I hated math, and I hated the counting chart ten times more than I hated math. All year Mrs. Pershun had forced us to slowly count with her as her fat finger made a path from one number to the next. And there it was, sitting right in front of me, like it was begging me to take it. I knew then it had to be mine—not because I wanted to own it, but because I wanted to hold it in my hands and make Mrs. Pershun watch me tear it up.

As my classmates walked away with their candy, I waited by the side of the table to see if anyone else had the same idea as me. But it seemed like most of them had already forgotten that Mrs. Pershun was a liar and a horrible person. They were happy to have chocolate, even if it was in place of the trip to Florida. Only one other person stood at the table—Jimi. He looked at me, then down at the counting chart, and then back at me. I could tell from the way his blue eyes jumped around that we were thinking the same thing. Without saying a word,

Jimi and I reached down and each grabbed a corner of the chart. We walked with it toward the front of the classroom.

"What're you going to do with that?" Jenny asked as we zigzagged between desks and over backpacks. Neither of us said a word.

When we reached a spot several feet in front of Mrs. Pershun's desk, Jimi and I stopped. I whispered to him, "Let's tear it up." He nodded like it was the only thing to do.

The smooth white cardboard felt cold in my hands. The chart was three feet long and almost two feet wide, and weighed more than it looked like it would. Its shiny surface was covered with lines and squiggles in every color. When my classmates saw us standing there, they stopped playing their games and walked toward the front of the room.

As the afternoon sun painted the spot on the floor by us white, Jimi and I stood in front of Mrs. Pershun and ripped the counting chart in half down the center. We each took a half and tore it, over and over again, until all that was left was a few pieces of cardboard on the checkered floor and a tiny corner in each of our hands.

By the time we finished, everyone in the class was standing up and cheering, the way they did when we played soccer in gym class and someone scored a goal. We were the two quiet kids who never got in any trouble, and they looked surprised that we were the ones being bad. But Mrs. Pershun didn't think it was as funny as they did. She stared daggers at us, the kind of look you feel all over your skin. Her body galloped toward us so fast I almost cried out. When she got to the front of the room, Mrs. Pershun's face scrunched into a red ball like a fat tomato. She was the kind of mad my mom was when she came home and saw me playing tennis in the living room, the kind of mad that starts in the brain and jumps to the mouth before the face is ready for it. Her body stood over us like an elephant, and she snatched the pieces of cardboard from our hands.

"This was extremely disrespectful," she yelled, pointing at the two of us with the larger white piece. "You are ungrateful children," she added, then sighed. She let the pieces of cardboard fall to the ground and put her hands on her hips.

Normally, when a grownup yelled at me, a prickly ball formed in my throat and I had to use all my energy to keep it from reaching my tear factory. My face would get the kind of hot it got when I was sun burnt, and I'd wish I was invisible forever. But not this time. As Mrs. Pershun stood there yelling at us, all I could think about was her elbow fat and the way it hung below the sleeves on her shirt and gathered at the bone like a folded ball of dough. I didn't hear the rest of what she said; every time she moved her arms and pointed at us, the jiggly fat bounced back and forth like it was clapping for itself. I tried not to smile as I thought about how Mrs. Pershun probably didn't understand the difference between "being disrespectful" and "teaching her something."

Contributor Bios

Thomas Burke is the Program Manager of the Chinua Achebe Center for African Literature and Languages at Bard College. In the past he served as Director of Summer Literary Seminars in Kenya, Assistant Director of SLS in Russia, and as the Event and Promotions Manager at *Words without Borders,* an online magazine of international literature in translation. He received an MFA from UMASS and his work has appeared in *Tin House, The Brooklyn Rail* and *Matrix,* among other places, and is forthcoming in the *St. Petersburg Review.*

Anthony D'Aries received the 2010 PEN New England Discovery Award in Nonfiction and served as Randolph College's 2011 Emerging Writer-in-Residence. His work has appeared in *The Literary Review* and *Solstice.*

Tammy Dietz is writer of fiction and nonfiction. She writes short stories, articles and essays. She is working on a novel and is the Senior Nonfiction Editor at *Silk Road Review.* Tammy is also a wife, a mother, an instructional designer at Microsoft, and a part-time liberal arts professor at DeVry University. She lives near Seattle.

Terri Elders, LCSW, lives in the country near Colville WA with two dogs and three cats. Her stories have been published in multiple editions of *Chicken Soup for the Soul, A Cup of Comfort, HCI's Ultimate, Literary Cottage Heroes* and *Patchwork Path.*

Tiffanie Gabrielse is a graduate of the University of Massachusetts at Dartmouth and is a columnist for *Encore Magazine* based in Wilmington, North Carolina. Her memoir is scheduled to be released Fall 2012, published by Plume. She and her husband are stationed at Camp Lejeune.

Julie Geen is a freelance writer, mother of two, and a substitute teacher. She lives in rural Virginia, and has been published in the local rags and the anthology *Ask Me about My Divorce* (Seal Press, 2009), although she did not end up getting that divorce. She also writes screenplays and is pretty sure she's going to Hollywood one day.

Corey Ginsberg studied creative writing at Carnegie Mellon University and Florida International University. Her work has most recently appeared in *Front Porch*, *Subtropics*, *The Cream City Review*, *The Los Angeles Review*, *Compass Rose*, and *The Writer*, among others. She currently lives in Miami and works as a freelance writer.

Angela M. Graziano's work has appeared in multiple print and online publications including *Apple Valley Review, Ariel, Design Sponge, Dislocate, Lost,* and *Portal Del Sol,* among others. She is the founding editor of www.SomethingGreenEvents. Blogspot.com, a popular eco party-planning blog. Her first memoir, *A Vision of Neon,* is forthcoming from Serving House Books.

Valley Haggard lives in Richmond, Virginia with her

husband and six-year-old son. A freelance writer who teaches creative writing, she has been the book editor for Richmond's alternative newspaper, *Style Weekly*, since 2004. Visit her at www.valleyhaggard.com.

Amanda Kingsbury worked as a travel, lifestyle, and arts/entertainment editor for newspapers in Arizona, Texas, North Carolina, and Indiana. She's currently the editor of an arts and entertainment weekly in Indianapolis, where she lives with her husband, daughter and cats in an old house frequently invaded by "sprickets" (creatures that look like a cross between spiders and crickets).

Jillian Lauren is the author of the *New York Times* bestselling memoir, *Some Girls: My Life in a Harem* and the novel, *Pretty*. She has an MFA from Antioch University and her writing has appeared in *The New York Times*, *The Paris Review Daily*, *Vanity Fair*, *Flaunt Magazine* and *Opium Magazine*, among others. She lives in Los Angeles with her husband and son.

Tambre Leighn, M.A., C.Ht., is an award winning documentary film producer. The loss of her mother as a teenager, and subsequent death of her husband less than ten years into their marriage, inspired Tambre to follow a new path. She recently launched her coaching business (coachingbytambre.com) to help others transform their grief and find the path to creating lives filled with passion and lived on purpose.

Jennifer Levy is a writer and life-long Baltimorian. Having worked in Maryland politics for the last decade, Jennifer's writing experience has been technical and dry in nature. Today, a stay-at-home mom, she is now learning to write for pleasure, exercising her voice in a more honest and social arena.

Jennifer D. Munro's work has appeared in many journals and anthologies, including *Best American Erotica*; *The Bigger the Better the Tighter the Sweater: 21 Funny Women on Beauty and Body Image*; and *Secrets and Confidences: The Complicated Truth about Women's Friendships*. Her published fiction is collected in *The Erotica Writer's Husband and Other Stories*. Visit her website at www.munrojd.com.

Jennifer Rhodes earned her MFA from Antioch University, Los Angeles and has had work featured in *The Battered Suitcase, The Citron Review* and Nerve.com among others. She is a writer and amateur pole dancer whose big mouth coupled with a complete absence of good judgment makes her a liability in most professional and social situations.

Marcy Sheiner has published many essays and feature stories on disability and other topics. *Perfectly Normal,* her memoir about giving birth to a child with hydrocephalus, is available on iUniverse.com. You can read her blog at http://www.marcys.wordpress.com. She is currently working on several projects, including a memoir of mother/daughterhood.

David Henry Sterry is an author, performer, educator, activist, and a man who hasn't worn matching socks in 20 years. David is the author of 12 books, the first of which was published in 2001, the latest of which is *The Essential Guide To Getting Your Book Published* (Workman, 2010). Prior to becoming an author, David was a professional actor and screenwriter.

Jennifer Tress' creative nonfiction and pop culture commentary has appeared in magazines including *Bitch* and *Young Money*. She is in the process of completing her first collection of humorous, true life stories and appears in east coast storytelling events where she performs her work. For more information, published pieces and show videos, go to yourenotprettyenough.com.

Leslie Tucker is a Detroit escapee, now living on the side of a South Carolina Mountain and refuses to divulge its exact location. She is an avid hiker and zip-liner, a dedicated yogi, and achieved Life Master status in ACBL Sanctioned Bridge last year. She is completing a collection of memoiric essays and prefers not to share more biographical data and spoil her story. She has degrees and business and music.

Amy Yelin's work has appeared in the *Gettysburg Review*, *The Baltimore Review*, *Literary Mama*, on WEKU (an NPR station), and in the *Boston Globe* and the *Globe Magazine*. Her essay "Torn" was a notable essay of 2006 in the *Best American Essays 2007*. She has an MFA in creative writing from Lesley University.

Essays by **J.W. Young** have been anthologized by Random House and Dzanc books. Her work has appeared in *Memoir (and)*, *Damselfly Press*, and *The Apple Valley Review*. She earned her MFA from Ole Miss, and currently teaches writing at Middle Georgia College.

About the Editors

Cara Bruce is the editor of *Viscera*, *Best Fetish Erotica*, and *Best Bisexual Women's Erotica*. She is the co-author of *The First Year - Hepatitis C* and *Horny? San Francisco*. Her short stories have been published in dozens of anthologies including *Best American Erotica*, *Best Women's Erotica 2000 – 2004*, the *Mammoth Book of New Erotica*, *Pills, Chills, Thrills and Heartache* and many more. She has been published in *The San Francisco Bay Guardian*, *Playgirl*, *Bust*, the *McClathy-Tribune*, and more. For more information: www.carabruce.com.

Shawna Kenney is the author of *Imposters* and the award-winning memoir *I Was a Teenage Dominatrix*. Her work has appeared in *Bust*, *Ms.*, *Juxtapoz*, the *Florida Review*, the *Indy Star* and various other outlets. For more information see www.shawnakenney.com.